Understanding Elections

What's Your **VOTE?**

Author

Torrey Maloof

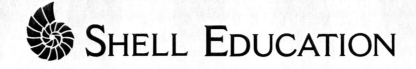
SHELL EDUCATION

Standards

To view how this information meets national and state standards, scan the QR code or visit our website at http://www.shelleducation.com and follow the on-screen instructions.

Publishing Credits

Corinne Burton, M.A.Ed., *President*; Emily R. Smith, M.A.Ed., *Content Director*; James D. Anderson, M.S.Ed., *Editor*; Grace Alba Le, *Multimedia Designer*; Stephanie Bernard, *Assistant Editor*; Don Tran, *Production Artist*

Image Credits

p. 11 malerapaso/iStockphoto; p. 12, 14 Chad Thompson; p. 15 LOC [LC-USZ62-19234]; p. 26 National Archives; p. 37 Pete Souza & Lawrence Jackson, The White House; p. 48 recreated by Tim Bradley from LOC image [LC-USZ62-116449]; p. 59 top left LOC [LC-DIG-highsm-03812], bottom right [LC-USZ62-128620] , p. 70 Teresa Azevedo/Shutterstock.com; p. 81 AP (Associated Press); p. 92 © Bettmann/CORBIS; p. 103 LOC [LC-USZ62-118572]; p.111 Kevin Dietsch/UPI/Newscom; p. 114 John F. Kennedy Presidential Library and Museum; p. 117 [LC-USZ62-34274] Library of Congress; Border Image nick73/iStockphoto; Layout Elements edge69/iStockphoto, sgursozlu/iStockphoto, marigold_88/iStockphoto, Yuri_Arcurs/iStockphoto; Illustrations, Timothy J. Bradley/Monique Dominguez/Evan Ferrell/Travis Hanson/Shutterstock

Standards

© 2004 Mid-continent Research for Education and Learning (McREL)

© Copyright 2010. National Governors Association Center for Best Practices and Council of Chief State School Officers. All rights reserved.

Shell Education
5301 Oceanus Drive
Huntington Beach, CA 92649-1030
http://www.shelleducation.com
ISBN 978-1-4258-1352-9
© 2015 Shell Education Publishing, Inc.

★ ★ ★ Table of Contents ★ ★ ★

★ ★ ★ The Importance of Civic Education ★ ★ ★

★ ★ ★ ★ ★ ★ ★ ★ ★ ★ ★ ★ ★ ★ ★ ★ ★ ★ ★

> "Young people must learn how to participate in a democracy."
> —*Constitutional Rights Foundation 2000*

It is the responsibility of those living in the United States to understand how civics relates to them. By being able to participate in a democracy, citizens can affect the nation and its well-being. Therefore, it is necessary for students to learn and understand civics. The National Council for the Social Studies (2010) states that social studies curricula should include opportunities to study "the ideals, principles, and practices of citizenship in a democratic republic." By learning civics, students can be committed to addressing social and government issues in a constructive way. However, in order to do this, students must understand the country and communities in which they live.

According to the National Standards for Civics and Government (Center for Civic Education 2014), the following are the organizing questions around which civic education should be based:

I. What is government and what should it do?

II. What are the basic values and principles of American democracy?

III. How does the government established by the Constitution embody the purposes, values, and principles of American democracy?

IV. What is the relationship of the United States to other nations and to world affairs?

V. What are the roles of the citizen in American democracy?

Teachers need to help students understand and respond to these civic questions so that students can apply their knowledge later in life when responding to daily events as adults in a democracy. Experiences during the K–12 school years lay the foundation for students to be able to evaluate situations and defend positions on public issues as well as influence civic life through working and managing conflict (Constitutional Rights Foundation 2000).

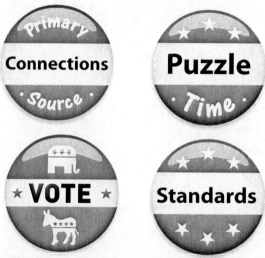

★ ★ ★ The Importance of Civic Education *(cont.)* ★ ★ ★

The lessons in this book bring about the following benefits and skills:

- increased written and oral communication

- working knowledge of government and democracy

- interest in current events

- higher likelihood of consistent voting and voting on issues rather than personality when an adult

- increased ability to clearly articulate opinions

- tolerance of differing opinions

- knowledge of how to make decisions even when others do not agree

- increased political and civic activeness

- appreciation of the importance and complexity of government

- increased civic attitude (Carnegie Corporation 2003)

In order for teachers to be effective, civic education needs to be recognized as a key aspect of today's curriculum. All of the aforementioned skills contribute to the goal of becoming a well-rounded, contributing, responsible, and civic-minded member of society outside of the classroom. However, these skills take time to develop and need to be integrated into the curriculum beginning in kindergarten and extending through 12th grade to be ultimately effective (Quigley 2005). Research suggests that children start to develop social responsibility and interest in politics before the age of nine. The way students are taught about social issues, ethics, and institutions in elementary school matters a great deal for their civic development (Kirlin 2005). Therefore, teachers have a responsibility to students to provide them with the activities necessary to learn these skills throughout their education.

★ ★ ★ ★ ★ ★ ★

> "[C]hildren start to develop social responsibility and interest in politics before the age of nine."

Civic education can be taught both formally and informally. Intentional formal lessons imbedded in the curriculum give students a clear understanding of government and politics and the historical context for those ideas. This instruction should avoid teaching rote facts and give as much real-life context as possible.

Informal curriculum refers to how teachers, staff, and the school climate can lead by example and illustrate to students how a working civic community operates (Quigley 2005). When adult role models portray and promote responsible civic engagement, students have a greater conceptual understanding of the formal, civic-based curriculum and how it relates to everyday life.

★ ★ ★ How to Use This Book ★ ★ ★

Overarching Themes

The lessons in this book cover three overarching themes, or units, that take students through the election process.

- **What Is a Presidential Election?**—This unit lays the foundation for elections. Students will make connections between rules and laws, learn about leadership, the importance of voting, and the characteristics of political parties.

- **Elect Me!**—In this unit, students will learn about the road to election day, characteristics of good leaders, and the responsibilities of leadership from national conventions to campaigning.

- **And the Winner Is...**—Students will experience the voting process and will learn about ballot counting and Inauguration Day in this unit.

Activities in this Book

The lessons in this book are divided into three sections. Each section is designed to engage student interest and enhance student knowledge of the lesson topic.

Paired-Texts Reading and Activities

Using paired fiction and nonfiction texts can be an engaging way to introduce a topic to students and allow them to compare and contrast various types of text. By pairing the texts, a connection is created between the content of both. Students may gravitate in interest toward one type of text—fiction or nonfiction. Presenting similar information in both types of text allows one passage to help build background knowledge while the other passage focuses on reinforcing that knowledge and building interest. Students will use graphic organizers to arrange their thoughts and participate in active learning opportunities with their peers.

Primary Source Connection

Using primary sources gives a unique view of history that other ways of teaching history are unable to do. Primary sources include newspaper articles, diaries, letters, drawings, photographs, maps, government documents, and other items created by people who experienced past events firsthand. Primary sources show students the subjective side of history, as many authors that experienced the same event often retell it in completely different ways. These resources also show students how events affected the lives of those who lived them. Primary sources make history real for students. As students view these historical items, they are then able to analyze the events from various points of view and biases. Each lesson contains a photograph or a document from election history.

★ ★ ★ **How to Use This Book** (cont.) ★ ★ ★

Activities in this Book (cont.)

Puzzle Time!

These are opportunities for students to practice content and problem-solving skills and to increase student engagement and interest in the lesson topic. Puzzles allow students to have fun while they reflect on what they have learned during the lesson. Students decode secret messages, use addition to create hidden images, find their way through fun mazes, and more!

Culminating Activity

This engaging activity is included to demonstrate students' overall knowledge of the election process and allow them to take part in a fun classroom election.

References Cited

Carnegie Corporation of New York and The Center for Information & Research on Civic Learning & Engagement. 2003. The Civic Mission of Schools. http://civicmission. s3.amazonaws.com/118/f7/1/172/2003_Civic_Mission_of_Schools_Report.pdf.

Center for Civic Education. 2014. National Standards for Civics and Government. http://www.civiced.org/standards.

Constitutional Rights Foundation. 2000. Fostering Civic Responsibility Through Service Learning. http://www.crf-usa.org/service-learning-network/8-1-fostering-civic-responsibility.html.

Kirlin, Mary. 2005. Promising Approaches for Strengthening Civic Education. White paper from the California Campaign for the Civic Mission of Schools http://www.cms-ca.org/CMS%20white%20paper%20final.pdf.

National Council for the Social Studies. 2010. *National Curriculum Standards for Social Studies: A Framework for Teaching, Learning, and Assessment*. Washington, D.C.: NCSS.

Quigley, C. N. 2005. The Civic Mission of the Schools: What Constitutes an Effective Civic Education? Paper presented at Education for Democracy: The Civic Mission of the Schools, Sacramento, CA. http://www.civiced.org/pdfs/sacramento0805.pdf

Choosing a Leader

Standards

☑ Students will know that promoting justice is one of the fundamental purposes of law in American society.

☑ Students will analyze fiction and nonfiction texts and synthesize the information in a variety of ways.

Paired Texts Reading and Activities

★ **Election Day!** (page 10)—Read the fictional story on page 10 to students. Then, have students reread the story in pairs. Next, have a class discussion about why voting for a president is a big decision. Have them pair-share times they had to make big decisions or choices. Have volunteers share their stories.

★ **What Is an Election?** (pages 11–12)—Read the informational text on page 11 aloud while students follow along. Then, have students read the text and use pencils to circle words they would like to clarify. Once they finish reading, work as a class to clarify any words students found confusing. Next, have students individually complete page 12. When students have finished, go over the answers as a class.

★ **Election Day Details** (page 13)— Have students use information from the fictional story and the informational text to answer the questions on page 13. Then, have them share their answers with peers.

★ **Election Day Step-by-Step** (page 14)—With this activity, students will use the words in the word bank to complete the sentences that describe the steps a person takes on Election Day. Then, they will cut out the pictures that show the steps at the bottom of the page and place them in the correct order. This activity can be done individually, in pairs, or in small groups. When students have finished, go over the answers as a class.

Choosing a Leader *(cont.)*

Primary Source Connection

★ **Fair Elections Primary Source**
(pages 15–16)—Study the primary source on page 15 with students. Read the background information to them. Tell students that a long time ago, African Americans were not allowed to vote and that this was unfair. Explain that today, all citizens that are at least 18 years old can vote and this is more fair. Have students work in pairs to complete page 16. Go over the directions of this page and clarify key vocabulary words students may not know, such as *citizen*.

Puzzle Time!

★ **Fill It In! Vocabulary Puzzle**
(page 17)—Students will enjoy completing this puzzle that challenges them to fill in the missing letters in the vocabulary words to find the answer to the question.

★ **Calculate and Color Puzzle**
(page 18)—Students will have fun solving addition problems and coloring the picture to find the hidden answer to the Election Day question.

Answer Key

What Is an Election? (page 12)

Election Day Details (page 13)
1. Election day is in November on the first Tuesday after the first Monday
2. They go to the polling place.
3. A ballot is a list of people who want to be president.
4. The votes are counted when everyone is done voting.

Bonus: Elections are fair because everyone has the right to vote.

Election Day Step-by-Step (page 14)
1. polling place
2. ballot
3. votes
4. ballot box

Fill It In! Vocabulary Puzzle (page 17)
1. leader
2. fair
3. polling place
4. election
5. vote
6. ballot
7. president

Answer: Lincoln

Calculate and Color Puzzle (page 18)

vote

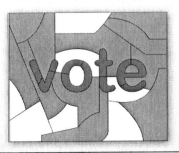

★★★ Election Day! ★★★

It is November. It is Tuesday. It is Election Day! Eva is excited. Her mom is going to vote. Her mom will vote for a new president!

Eva gets to go with her mom. The two of them drive to the polling place. This is where Eva's mom will make a choice. She will choose who she thinks will be the best leader. She will fill out a ballot. Then, she will turn it in.

In the car, Eva asks, "Mom, this is so fun! Why didn't we do this yesterday?"

Eva's mom says, "Election Day is always in November. It is on the first Tuesday after the first Monday. That is the only day the polls are open."

At the polling place, Eva's mom gets a ballot. The ballot has a list of names. It shows who is running for president. She takes the ballot into a voting booth. She makes her choice. She chooses who she wants to be the next president. It is a big choice! Next, she drops her ballot in a box. That's it! Eva's mom has voted!

Eva can't wait until she is older. Then, she can vote, too. And she can't wait to see who wins the election!

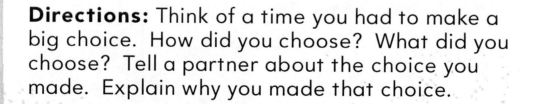

Directions: Think of a time you had to make a big choice. How did you choose? What did you choose? Tell a partner about the choice you made. Explain why you made that choice.

★ ★ ★ **What Is an Election?** ★ ★ ★

Do you know what an election is? It is a fair way to pick laws. And it is a fair way to choose a leader. The president is the leader of the whole country. A new president is chosen every four years. This happens on Election Day!

Election Day is in November. It is always on the first Tuesday after the first Monday. On this day, people go to a polling place.

First, they get a ballot. This is a list of people. These people want to be president.

Next, they go into a voting booth. Then, they vote! They pick a leader.

After that, they turn in their ballot. They drop it into a box. Or they push a button on a computer.

Last, the votes are counted. The person with the most votes wins!

Everyone has the right to vote. This is why elections are fair. They are just.

★ ★ ★ **What Is an Election?** (cont.) ★ ★ ★

Directions: An election is a fair way to make a choice. When something is fair, it is equal for everyone. Read the sentences below. Color the pictures that are fair. Draw a big *X* on the pictures that are unfair.

Sal does not share.

Gigi takes a turn as line leader.

Everyone rides the bus.

Only tall kids can buy ice cream.

#51352—Understanding Elections   © Shell Education

★ ★ ★ Election Day Details ★ ★ ★

Directions: Use the information from *Election Day!* and *What Is an Election?* to answer the questions below. You can draw or write your answers.

1. What month and day of the week is Election Day?	**2.** Where do people go to vote on Election Day?
3. What is a ballot?	**4.** What happens after everyone is done voting?

☆ ☆

Bonus: Why are elections fair?

_____

_____

★ ★ ★ Election Day Step-by-Step ★ ★ ★

Directions: Write the steps a person takes on Election Day. Use the words from the Word Bank to complete the sentences. Then, cut out the pictures below and place them in the correct order.

> **Word Bank**
>
> ballot   ballot box   polling place   votes

Step 1: She goes to the _____ .

Step 2: She gets a _____ .

Step 3: She _____ or chooses a leader.

Step 4: She puts her ballot in the _____ .

★★★ **Fair Elections Primary Source** ★★★

Primary Source Background Information

This picture is from 1867. It shows an African American man. He is voting for the first time. A long time ago, African Americans could not vote. Women could not vote. American Indians could not vote either. This was not fair. Things were not equal. Many brave people fought for equal rights. It took many years. Today, every citizen over 18 years old has the right to vote.

Alfred Rudolph Waud, Library of Congress

★ ★ ★ Fair Elections Primary Source (cont.) ★ ★ ★

Directions: Can you think of something that is fair? Can you think of something that is unfair? Draw a picture for each.

Fair

Unfair

 #51352—Understanding Elections

★★★ Fill It In! Vocabulary Puzzle ★★★

Directions: Fill in the missing letters in the vocabulary words. Then, write the letters from the squares in order on the lines below to answer the question. Use the Word Bank to help you.

Word Bank

BALLOT	POLLING PLACE	LEADER
ELECTION	FAIR PRESIDENT	VOTE

1. [ ] E __ D E R

2. F __ [ ] R

3. P O L __ I [ ] G __ L __ C E

4. E __ E [ ] T I __ N

5. V [ ] T __

6. B __ [ ] L __ T

7. P __ E __ I D E [ ] T

Question: This leader lost lots of elections before he was finally elected president. He loved cats and hated being called "Abe." Who was he?

Answer: __ __ __ __ __ __ __

★★★ Calculate and Color Puzzle ★★★

Directions: Solve the problems below. Using the key, color the picture to find the answer to the question.

Key

| 8 = red | 2 = white | 10 = blue |

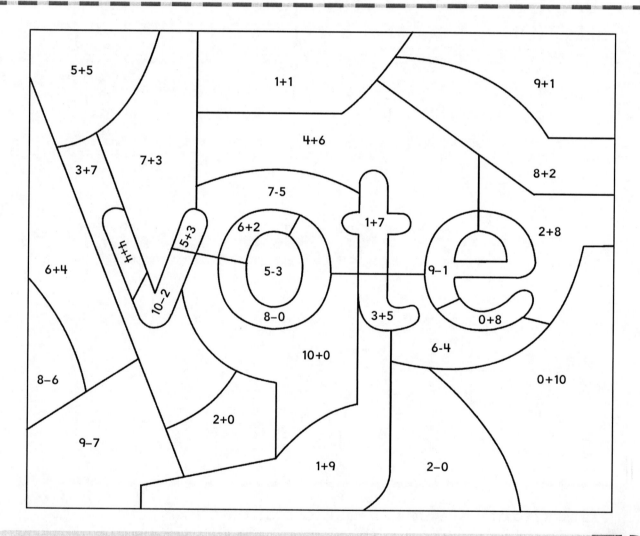

Question: What do people do on Election Day?

Answer: ___ ___ ___ ___

#51352—Understanding Elections

The Rules and Laws

Standards

 Students will know that a good rule or law solves a specific problem, is fair, and "does not go too far."

 Students will analyze fiction and nonfiction texts and synthesize the information in a variety of ways.

Paired Texts Reading and Activities

★ **Rules and Laws** (pages 21–22)— Read the poem on page 21 aloud to students. Have students reread the poem in pairs and think of rules that they follow. Then, have them play charades with partners to act out their rules and guess their partners' rules. Select a few students to act out their rules in front of the class. Next, have students individually complete page 22. If students are struggling to think of laws, brainstorm as a class and create a list for students to choose from. Have volunteers share their responses with the class.

★ **What It Takes** (page 23)—Read the informational text on page 23 aloud while students follow along. Then, have students read the text individually or in pairs. Once students are finished, have a brief class discussion about why laws are created. Then, have groups of students choose laws and create newscasts about those laws. Talk with students about what makes a good news report. Ask volunteers to share their newscasts with the class.

★ **Listing the Laws** (page 24)— Students will use information from both the poem and the informational text to complete the T-chart on this page. After students have completed the assignment, draw the T-chart on the board and have students share their answers.

★ **My Elections Law** (page 25)—With this activity, students will write laws about elections that they would like to see added to the Constitution. This activity can be done individually, in pairs, or in small groups. When students have finished, go over as a class the laws students wrote.

The Rules and Laws (cont.)

Primary Source Connection

★ **Too Young to Vote Primary Source** (pages 26–27)—Study the primary source on page 26 with students. Read the background information to them. Have a brief class discussion on what an opinion is. Encourage students to really think about how they feel about the voting age law. Tell students they need to have reasons to support their opinions. Then, have them work in pairs to complete page 27.

Puzzle Time!

★ **Rules and Laws Vocabulary Puzzle** (page 28)—Students will enjoy completing this crossword puzzle made from the vocabulary words for this lesson.

★ **Voting Age Puzzle** (page 29)—Students will have fun solving this tricky math puzzle. They start with a number and follow a series of math computations to find the answer to the puzzle. **Note:** If this activity is too difficult for younger students, complete the first five steps as a class. This will provide the correct answer, as well.

Answer Key

Listing the Laws (page 24)

Voter	President
be over 18 years old	be 35 years or older
be a U.S. citizen	be born in the United States
have a U.S. address	live in the United States for 14 years or more

My Elections Law (page 25)

Students' laws will vary but should be fair.

Too Young To Vote Primary Source (page 27)

Students' posters and slogans will vary but should clearly state their feelings about the law.

Rules and Laws Vocabulary Puzzle (page 28)

Across
1. document
4. rules
6. laws

Down
2. Constitution
3. rights
5. equal

What's the Number? Puzzle (page 29)
1. Begin with the number 8.
2. 10
3. 5
4. 15
5. 18
6. 10
7. 1
8. 8
9. 4
10. 13
11. 18

You must be **18** years old to vote!

★ ★ ★ **Rules and Laws** ★ ★ ★
by Dona Rice

Let's follow the rules!
Let's follow the rules!
Rule followers rule—
Let's follow the rules!

Parents set the rules
at home—
Let's follow the rules!
Rules help us all to get
along—
Let's follow the rules!

Teachers set the rules
at school—
Let's follow the rules!
Rules help us all stay
extra cool—
Let's follow the rules!

Let's follow the rules!
Let's follow the rules!
Rule followers rule—
Let's follow the rules!

Some rules keep us safe
from harm—
Let's follow the rules!
Like crosswalks and a
smoke alarm—
Let's follow the rules!

Congress sets our rules
called laws—
Let's follow the rules!
They keep us safe and
well because—
We follow the rules!

Let's follow the rules!
Let's follow the rules!
Rule followers rule—
Let's follow the rules!

Some laws we use so we
can vote—
Let's follow the rules!
Know the laws and take
good note—
Let's follow the rules!

Laws help us know just
what to do—
Let's follow the rules!
Maybe you can be a
lawmaker, too!—
Let's follow the rules!

Let's follow the rules!
Let's follow the rules!
Rule followers rule—
Let's follow the rules!

★ ★ ★ Rules and Laws (cont.) ★ ★ ★

Directions: Draw or write one rule you follow at home and one rule you follow at school. Then, draw or write one of our country's laws that you follow.

Home

School

Country

#51352—Understanding Elections

★ ★ ★ **What It Takes** ★ ★ ★

Can kids vote? Yes! They can vote for a class leader. Or they can vote for what to eat for dinner. But they cannot vote for the next president of the United States. This is against the law.

The United States Constitution is a document. It states the laws for our country. It says what we can do. It says what we cannot do. It also lists the laws for elections.

It says that everyone has the right to vote. But you have to be over 18 years old. You must be a U.S. citizen. You have to give your address. This proves you live here.

Can anyone be president? No. There are laws about that, too! The laws state that you have to be 35 years old or older. You need to have been born in the United States. Also, you must have lived here for 14 years or more. If all these musts are met, then you can be the president!

The laws in the Constitution help keep elections equal. They help keep them fair for all.

Directions: Get in a group of three or four. Work with your group to choose one of the laws from the text. Make a list of why that law may be important. Then, pretend you are newscasters. Create a news report that tells people about the law and why it is important. Act out the newscast as a team for your class.

Name _____ Date _____

★★★ **Listing the Laws** ★★★

Directions: List the laws a voter must follow under *Voter*. Then under *President*, list the requirements a person must meet to be president.

Voter	President

★ ★ ★ My Elections Law ★ ★ ★

Directions: Write a new election law that you want added to the Constitution. Make sure your law is fair for everyone. Draw a picture that has to do with your law.

★★★ Too Young to Vote Primary Source ★★★

Primary Source Background Information

This picture was taken on August 3, 1965. It shows a young Marine. He was fighting in the Vietnam War. Back then, you could join the armed forces if you were 18 years old. But you could not vote. To vote, you had to be 21. Pictures like this one were used to help change the law. People thought 18-year-olds should get to vote. They would say, "If they are old enough to fight, they are old enough to vote." The law was changed in 1971. Now 18-year-olds can vote!

National Archives

★ ★ ★ Too Young to Vote Primary Source *(cont.)* ★ ★ ★

Directions: Do you think 18-year-olds should be allowed to vote? Do you think changing the law was the right thing to do? Draw a poster that shows how you feel about the law.

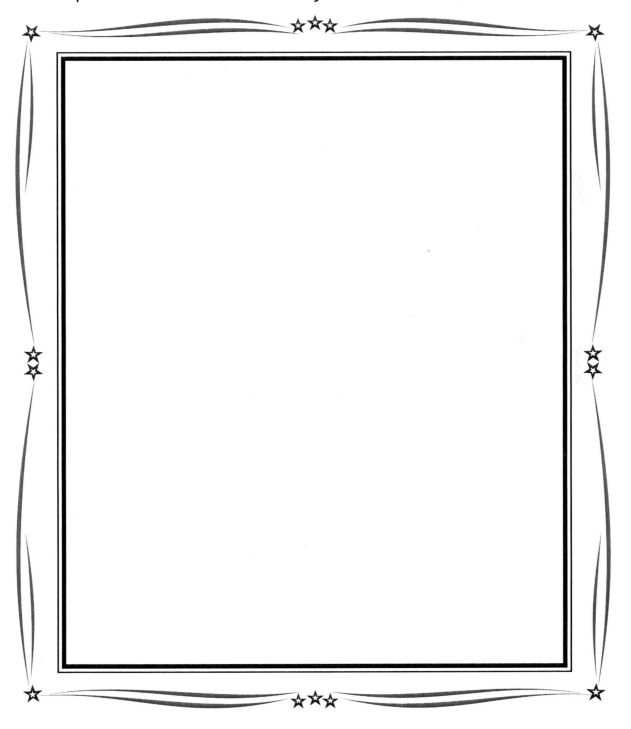

★★★ **Rules and Laws Vocabulary Puzzle** ★★★

Directions: Use the clues to complete the puzzle. You can use the words in the Word Bank to help you.

Word Bank

Constitution

document

equal

laws

rights

rules

Across

1. This is an official paper that gives information.

4. These tell you what you may or may not do.

6. These are rules for our country.

Down

2. This is the set of laws for our country.

3. Things people should be allowed to have or do.

5. This means it is the same for each person.

★★★ **Voting Age Puzzle** ★★★

Directions: Solve the problems below. Your last sum will be the answer to the puzzle below. The first one is done for you.

1. Begin with the number $\boxed{8}$

2. Add 2. ___8___ + 2 = ___10___

3. Subtract 5. ___10___ – 5 = _____

4. Add 10. _____ + 10 = _____

5. Add 3. _____ + 3 = _____

6. Subtract 8. _____ – 8 = _____

7. Subtract 9. _____ – 9 = _____

8. Add 7. _____ + 7 = _____

9. Subtract 4. _____ – 4 = _____

10. Add 9. _____ + 9 = _____

11. Add 5. _____ + 5 = $\boxed{}$

How old do you have to be to vote in an election?

You must be _____ years old to vote!

The Person in Charge

Standards

☑ Students will know the characteristics of a good leader (e.g., experience, determination, confidence, a desire to be a leader, the ability to solve problems creatively).

☑ Students will analyze fiction and nonfiction texts and synthesize the information in a variety of ways.

Paired Texts Reading and Activities

★ **Lincoln the Leader** (pages 32–33)—Read the historical fiction story on page 32 aloud to students. Model good fluency. Then, have them reread the story in pairs. Tell students to discuss their favorite parts of the story with their partners. Have them individually complete page 33. Ask volunteers to share their responses with the class.

★ **Leading Our Country** (page 34)—Read the informational text on page 34 aloud while students follow along. Then, have students read the text with pencils. Ask them to underline any words or sentences they do not understand. Once they finish rereading, have a brief class discussion about parts of the text they underlined. Then, have students fold large pieces of paper in half and make signs. On one side, they should show with drawings and text reasons why they would want to be president. On the other side, they should show reasons why they would not want to be president. Have volunteers share some of their reasons with the class.

★ **Being a President** (page 35)—Students will use information from both the story and the informational passage to complete the graphic organizer on this page. After students complete the assignment, draw the graphic organizer on the board and have students share their answers.

★ **If I Were President** (page 36)—With this activity, students will imagine they are the president of the United States. They will complete various sentence prompts to describe what they would do during their term. When students finish, have them share some of their responses with the class.

The Person in Charge (cont.)

Primary Source Connection

★ **White House Primary Source** (pages 37–38)—Study the photographs on page 37 with students. Read the background information to them. Have a brief class discussion on what the White House is. If students have seen or visited the White House, have them share their experiences with the class. Ask students to complete page 38 individually and share their first days as presidents.

Puzzle Time!

★ **Decode It Vocabulary Puzzle** (page 39)—Students will enjoy decoding this puzzle to create the vocabulary words for this lesson.

★ **Hidden Leader Puzzle** (page 40)—Students will have fun coloring this puzzle to create a famous leader.

Answer Key

Lincoln the Leader (page 33)

Student responses will vary but they should clearly express details on why the person is a great leader. Details could include the traits: hard working, fair, honest, and smart.

Being a President (page 35)

Answers will vary but may include the following:
- **Characteristics:** brave, smart, honest, knows a lot about history, knows about our country and the world, helps Americans, helps the country, treats people equally, good at solving problems, helps people get along, has experience
- **Responsibilities:** sign laws, in charge of the armed forces, meets with other leaders, helps countries get along with one another

Decode It Vocabulary Puzzle (page 39)
1. experience
2. responsibility
3. government
4. honest
5. smart

Hidden Leader Puzzle (page 40)

1	2	3	4	5	6	7	8	9	10
11	12	13	14	15	16	17	18	19	20
21	22	23	24	25	26	27	28	29	30
31	32	33	34	35	36	37	38	39	40
41	42	43	44	45	46	47	48	49	50
51	52	53	54	55	56	57	58	59	60
61	62	63	64	65	66	67	68	69	70
71	72	73	74	75	76	77	78	79	80
81	82	83	84	85	86	87	88	89	90
91	92	93	94	95	96	97	98	99	100

Abraham Lincoln

★ ★ ★ Lincoln the Leader ★ ★ ★

"Abe! Abe! Abraham Lincoln! Get over here right this instant. I need your help."

Young Abe did not hear his father yelling. He was too busy reading. Abe loved reading. He was leaning against a tree. Abe was lost in the words in the book.

"Put that book down and help me!" his father shouted. The angry man was now standing over his son.

Abe quickly scrambled to his feet, "Yes, Sir!"

For the rest of the day, Abe helped his father on the farm. But his mind was somewhere else. He was thinking about the book. It was about George Washington. Abe thought George was brave and smart.

"Father, don't you think President Washington was a great leader?" asked Abe.

"Sure," grumbled his father. "Keep working."

"I think he helped our country. And he helped the people in our country. I want to be like him when I grow up," Abe said gleefully.

"You're going to be a farmer when you grow up. Now, stop yapping and get back to work!" yelled his father.

But Abe's father was wrong. Abraham Lincoln would grow up to be one of the greatest presidents in history. He was honest and smart, and he treated people equally. He helped our country and its people.

★ ★ ★ **Lincoln the Leader** *(cont.)* ★ ★ ★

Directions: President Lincoln and President Washington were great leaders. Think about a leader you know. Write this person's name. Describe why this person is a great leader on the lines. Draw a picture of the person being a great leader.

_____
(name)

This person is a great leader because . . .

_____

_____

_____

_____

★★★ Leading Our Country ★★★

Do you know who leads our country? The leader is called the *president*. We, the people, pick the president. We do this every four years. It is a big choice. It is important. We vote for whom we think will be the best leader. We do this in elections.

Presidents need to be smart. They should know a lot about history. They must know a great deal about our country. They need to know about the world, too.

Presidents need to be honest. They should tell the truth. They must know how to solve problems. They should also be good at helping people get along.

Presidents need to have experience. This means they have already been good leaders. Most people who want to be president work for the government first.

Being president is a big job! Presidents have lots of responsibilities. They sign laws. These are the rules for our country. Presidents are also in charge of our armed forces. They keep our country safe. Presidents meet with leaders from other countries. They try to help countries get along.

Good presidents keep our country safe. They help make our country great. Do you want to be president someday?

Directions: Make a sign! Fold a piece of large paper in half. On one side, draw and write the reasons why you would want to be the president. On the other side, show the reasons you would not want to be president.

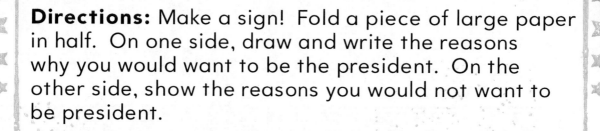

★★★ **Being a President** ★★★

Directions: Use both texts to complete the graphic organizer below. Write characteristics of a good president in the ovals on the left. Then, write responsibilities a president has in the ovals on the right.

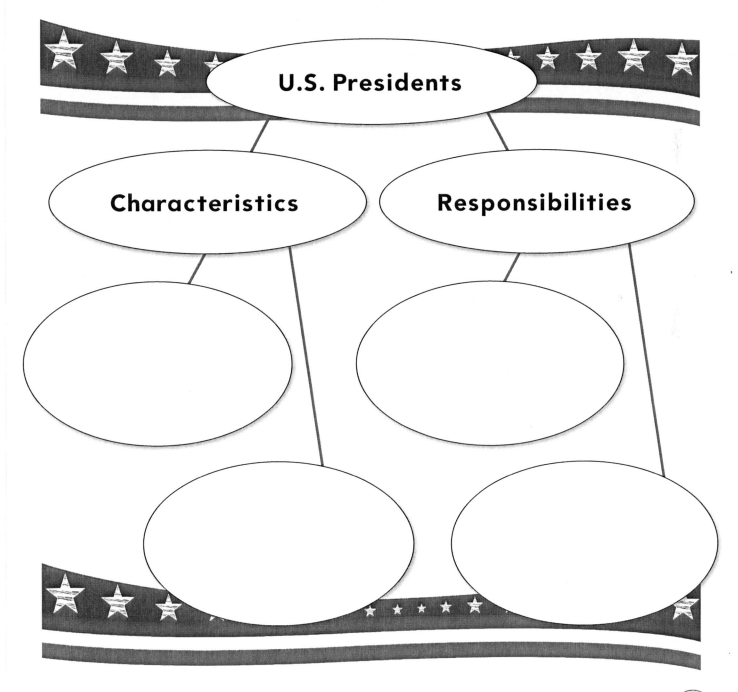

U.S. Presidents

Characteristics

Responsibilities

★★★ **If I Were President** ★★★

Directions: Pretend you are the president of the United States. What would you do? Finish the sentences and answer the question below.

If I Were President

I would be _____.

I would help _____.

I would change _____.

I would like _____.

I would not like _____.

What makes a good president?

_____

_____

_____

_____

★★★ White House Primary Source ★★★

Primary Source Background Information

The White House is where the president lives. It is also where the president works. George Washington chose the site for the White House, but he never got to live there. It took eight years to build the big house. In 1814, the British burned the White House down. It had to be rebuilt. The White House is huge! It has 132 rooms and 35 bathrooms. There is a movie theater and a basketball court. There is a playground. There is even a lawn where you can play volleyball.

Shutterstock (top left), Pete Souza & Lawrence Jackson, The White House (all others)

★ ★ ★ White House Primary Source (cont.) ★ ★ ★

Directions: Pretend you are the president. You just moved into the White House. What will you do during your first day in this big place? Will you swim? Will you work in your office? Will you watch a movie in the movie theater? Draw a picture about your first day in the White House. Then, write a sentence or two telling about it.

_____

_____

_____

★★★ Decode It Vocabulary Puzzle ★★★

Directions: Use the number chart below and the definitions to write the vocabulary words.

1 = A	2 = B	3 = C	4 = D	5 = E	6 = F	7 = G	8 = H	9 = I
10 = J	11 = K	12= L	13 = M	14 = N	15 = O	16 = P	17 = Q	18 = R
19 = S	20 = T	21 = U	22 = V	23 = W	24 = X	25 = Y	26 = Z	

1. skill or knowledge that you get by doing something

___ ___ ___ ___ ___ ___ ___ ___ ___ ___

  5   24   16   5   18   9   5   14   3   5

2. a duty or task that you need to do

___ ___ ___ ___ ___ ___ ___ ___ ___ ___ ___ ___ ___ ___

  18 5 19 16 15 14 19 9 2 9 12 9 20 25

3. the group of people who make decisions for our country

___ ___ ___ ___ ___ ___ ___ ___ ___ ___

  7   15   22   5   18   14   13   5   14   20

4. truthful

___ ___ ___ ___ ___ ___

  8   15   14   5   19   20

5. intelligent

___ ___ ___ ___ ___

  19   13   1   18   20

★★★ **Hidden Leader Puzzle** ★★★

Directions: Use the color key below to create one of our great leaders. When you are finished, write the name of the leader at the bottom of the page.

green: 67

red: 87, 88

brown: 54, 64, 74, 84, 94, 95, 96, 97, 98

peach: 55, 56, 57, 58, 65, 66, 68, 75, 76, 77, 78, 79, 85, 86

black: 4, 5, 6, 7, 8, 14, 15, 16, 17, 18, 24, 25, 26, 27, 28, 34, 35, 36, 37, 38, 43, 44, 45, 46, 47, 48, 49

1	2	3	4	5	6	7	8	9	10
11	12	13	14	15	16	17	18	19	20
21	22	23	24	25	26	27	28	29	30
31	32	33	34	35	36	37	38	39	40
41	42	43	44	45	46	47	48	49	50
51	52	53	54	55	56	57	58	59	60
61	62	63	64	65	66	67	68	69	70
71	72	73	74	75	76	77	78	79	80
81	82	83	84	85	86	87	88	89	90
91	92	93	94	95	96	97	98	99	100

Donkey or Elephant?

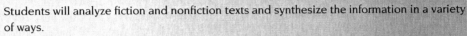

Standards

 Students will know examples of situations in which individuals are acting on their own (e.g., two friends decide to do something) and situations in which individuals' actions are directed by others (e.g., parents tell their children to do something).

 Students will analyze fiction and nonfiction texts and synthesize the information in a variety of ways.

Paired Texts Reading and Activities

★ **The Donkey and the Elephant** (pages 43–44)—Read the fable on page 43 aloud to students. Briefly discuss with the class what a fable is. Then, have students reread the fable in pairs and have them complete page 44. Go over the answers as a class.

★ **It's Party Time** (page 45)— Read the informational text on page 45 aloud while students follow along. Then, have them read the text with red and blue colored pencils. Ask students to circle the text that tells about the Republican Party in red. Have them circle the text that tells about the Democratic Party in blue. Explain that when people join a party, they tend to vote the way their party votes but they do not have to. Finally, have students draw pictures that tell about the Republican Party on one side of a sheet of paper and the Democratic Party on the other side.

Note for Teachers: At some point in this lesson, be sure to discuss third parties and their role in today's political processes.

★ **Which Party Is It?** (page 46)— Students will use information from the informational text to figure out which party the sentence is describing. They will draw a line from each sentence to the picture of the party symbol it matches. Go over the answers as a class, and discuss how this text relates to the fable.

★ **What Do I Believe?** (page 47)— With this activity, students will list what they believe about the role government should play in our lives.

Donkey or Elephant? (cont.)

Primary Source Connection

★ **Political Parties Primary Source**
(pages 48–49)—Study the primary
source on page 48 with students.
Read the background information
to them. Explain to students
what a political cartoon is. If
time permits, share additional
examples of political cartoons.
Then, have students complete
page 49 in pairs. Have volunteers
share the cartoons with the class.

Puzzle Time!

★ **Parties in Pieces Vocabulary
Puzzle** (page 50)—Students
will enjoy putting these puzzles
together to reveal the symbols for
the two political parties.

★ **Word Party Puzzle** (page 51)—
Students will have fun trying to
think of as many words as they can
that can be made from the words
Republican and *Democratic*.

Answer Key

The Donkey and the Elephant (page 44)

Characters	Setting
Donkey, Elephant	a circus
Problem	**Moral (lesson learned)**
the main tent at the circus catches fire	it's important to work as a team and help each other

Which Party Is It? (page 46)

Donkey	The government should provide services to its people.
Elephant	The government should be smaller.
Donkey	All citizens should have health care.
Elephant	There should be fewer taxes.

Bonus: Answers may include—"The Donkey and
Elephant" represents the two main political groups
in the United States. From the fable, each party can
learn that it is important to help each other even if
you do not always agree with each other.

Political Parties Primary Source (page 49)

Students' political cartoons will vary. Students
should be able to explain their cartoons.

Parties in Pieces Vocabulary Puzzle (page 50)

Republican   Democratic
Party   Party

Word Party Puzzle (page 51)

Possible answers:

Republican—public, per, can, I, pure, nail, nice,
pine, pan, lip, pile, care

Democratic—rate, more, core, rat, rate, trace, crate,
come, to, me, mode

★ ★ ★ The Donkey and the Elephant ★ ★ ★

Donkey and Elephant worked in a circus. They loved the circus. It was a fun job. But they did not like each other. They did not get along. They fought all the time. They did not believe in the same things.

One day, the two were having a big fight. Elephant stopped yelling for a moment. He smelled something in the air. Then, Donkey saw smoke. The two animals ran toward the smoke. They found the main circus tent on fire!

"What should we do?" cried Donkey.

Elephant was already trying to put out the fire. He was sucking up water with his long trunk from a nearby well. He was squirting it on the fire. But the fire was too fierce!

"Donkey what should we do? Our beloved circus is going to burn down!" shouted Elephant between squirts. "We need help!"

Donkey turned and ran. He ran all the way to the fire department. Elephant kept squirting water on the fire. It kept the fire from spreading and getting bigger. Donkey returned with firefighters. They put out the fire quickly.

Donkey and Elephant had saved the circus! That day, they realized they had something in common. They both loved the circus. It was their home. They would do anything to save it, even if that meant working together.

★ ★ ★ The Donkey and the Elephant *(cont.)* ★ ★ ★

Directions: Think about the fable. Use the fable to complete the chart below. Then, draw a picture that shows your favorite part of the fable.

Characters	Setting
_____	_____
_____	_____
Problem	**Moral (lesson learned)**
_____	_____
_____	_____
_____	_____
_____	_____

My favorite part is . . .

★★★ **It's Party Time!** ★★★

It is election time! You keep hearing the same two words. One word is *Republican*. The other word is *Democratic*. These are parties. But there are no cakes. There are no gifts. They are political parties.

There are many political parties. Two of these parties are larger than the rest.

The Republican Party's symbol is an elephant. They think people should make their own choices with their money. They believe the government should be smaller. And it should be smart with money. They believe there should be few taxes. They think our country should be safe and strong with a strong military.

The Democratic Party's symbol is a donkey. They believe in a strong government. They believe everyone should get a fair chance. They want to grow opportunities for people. They want all citizens to have health care. They think the government should provide services for the people in the country.

Both parties want to keep our country safe. They want our country to be strong. They both believe in freedom, strong education, and civil rights. Most people who run for president belong to one of these two parties.

Directions: Take a sheet of paper. On one side, draw pictures that tell about the Republican Party. On the back of the paper, draw pictures that tell about the Democratic Party. Explain your pictures to a partner.

★ ★ ★ **Which Party Is It?** ★ ★ ★

Directions: Draw a line from each sentence to the picture of the party symbol it matches.

The government should provide services to its people.

The government should be smaller.

All citizens should have health care.

There should be fewer taxes.

Bonus: How does "The Donkey and the Elephant" fable relate to political parties? What can each party learn from the fable?

_____

_____

_____

★ ★ ★ **What Do I Believe?** ★ ★ ★

Directions: Think about what you learned about political parties. They have different beliefs. What do you believe? What do you like about life in the United States? What would you like to change?

Things I think are important in the United States:

_____

_____

_____

_____

_____

Things I would like to change about the United States:

_____

_____

_____

_____

_____

★ ★ ★ Political Parties Primary Source ★ ★ ★

Primary Source Background Information

Political cartoons are popular! Artists find clever ways to talk about politics. They do this by drawing cartoons. The cartoon below is from 1962. The artist's name is Bruce Russell. This cartoon tells people to vote. The elephant's trunk makes the *R* in the word *register*. The donkey's ears make the letter *V* in the word *vote*. This way, the cartoon is for both Republicans and Democrats.

Recreated by Timothy J. Bradley from the original image by Bruce Russell

★ ★ ★ **Political Parties Primary Source** (cont.) ★ ★ ★

Directions: Think about what the Democratic Party and the Republican Party stand for. Now draw a political cartoon about one of the parties. Be sure to think of a title for your cartoon!

_____

(title)

★★★ Parties in Pieces Vocabulary Puzzle ★★★

Directions: Cut out the vocabulary words. Then, cut out the puzzle pieces. Put the pieces together to create two pictures. Place the correct vocabulary word under each puzzle.

★ ★ ★ **Word Party Puzzle** ★ ★ ★

Directions: How many words can you make from letters in the word *Republican*? How many words can you make from letters in the word *Democrat*? Use the letters in the two political parties to make as many words as you can. Ready, set, go!

REPUBLICAN	DEMOCRAT
bun	*come*

Who's in the Race?

Standards

☑ Students will know that a responsibility is a duty to do something or not to do something.

☑ Students will analyze fiction and nonfiction texts and synthesize the information in a variety of ways.

★ **The Best Day Ever!** (pages 54–55)—Read the diary entry on page 54 aloud to students. Model good fluency. Then, have students reread the diary entry in pairs. Have them complete page 55 independently. It is a body map in which students will write Abigail's thoughts and feelings. Ask volunteers to share their responses with the class.

★ **Who's Running?** (page 56)—Read the informational text on page 56 aloud while students follow along. Then, have students read the text with pencils. Ask them to circle what they feel is the most interesting part of the text. Have students work in pairs to create signs to take to a national convention.

★ **Detailed Balloons** (page 57)—Students will use information from both the informational text and the diary entry to list the details they learned about national conventions. Students can work individually, in pairs, or in small groups to complete the activity sheet. When students have finished, draw the graphic organizer on the board and fill in the balloons together as a class.

★ **Planning the Perfect Convention** (page 58)—Students will plan the perfect convention in this activity. Have a class discussion about the importance of being responsible. Ask students to share some of the responsibilities they have at home and school. Then, tell students they will pretend they are in charge of planning the next national convention. Tell them it is a big responsibility and that they will have to think and plan carefully. Have students work with partners to complete the questions and draw pictures of how their conventions will look.

Who's in the Race? *(cont.)*

Primary Source Connection

★ **Party Time! Primary Source** (pages 59–60)—Study the primary sources on page 59 with students. Read the background information to them. Then, have them complete page 60 in pairs. When students have finished, draw the Venn diagram on the board. Ask students to share their responses and write them on the diagram on the board.

Puzzle Time!

★ **Convention Crossword Vocabulary Puzzle** (page 61)—Students will enjoy solving this crossword puzzle that includes words about national conventions.

★ **Crazy Convention Puzzle** (page 62)—Students will have fun trying to find the hidden pictures in this silly picture of a crazy national convention.

Answer Key

The Best Day Ever! (page 55)

Student responses will vary, but should be relevant to the sights and sounds of a national convention.

Detailed Balloons (page 57)

Student answers will vary but may include the following details: they are like big parties; they last for days; they are shown on TV; people give speeches; each party announces who will run for president

Party Time! Primary Source (page 60)

2008: people are standing; people are celebrating; balloons are falling; there is a giant TV screen

Both: decorations; American flags; lots of people

1920: people are sitting; people are calm; people are looking at the camera; there are a few signs

Convention Crossword Vocabulary Puzzle (page 61)

Across	Down
2. speech	1. key
4. issues	3. convention
5. candidate	

Crazy Convention Puzzle (page 62)

★ ★ ★ The Best Day Ever! ★ ★ ★

Dear Diary,

You will never guess what happened to me today. It was so amazing! I get goose bumps just thinking about it. I can't stop smiling. I want to jump around the room! I want to dance! I want to sing! My party chose me! I get to run to be the next president of the United States of America!

I am so excited. I could not be happier. But now I'm starting to get nervous. I have to give the biggest speech I have ever given at the national convention. There will be over 80,000 people there. Plus, I will be on TV! I hope my speech is strong. I hope I don't mess up!

I have worked so hard to get here. I want to make my country proud. I want to help my country and its people. I want people to vote for me because they think I will be a great leader. I know I can be. I will be honest. I will work hard. I will help people get along. I will be strong and make good choices. I will keep our country safe.

I guess I should go practice my speech. Wish me luck!

Sincerely,

Abigail

★ ★ ★ **The Best Day Ever!** (cont.) ★ ★ ★

Directions: Abigail has to give a big speech. Pretend she just stepped on stage at the national convention to give her speech. Fill in the body map for Abigail.

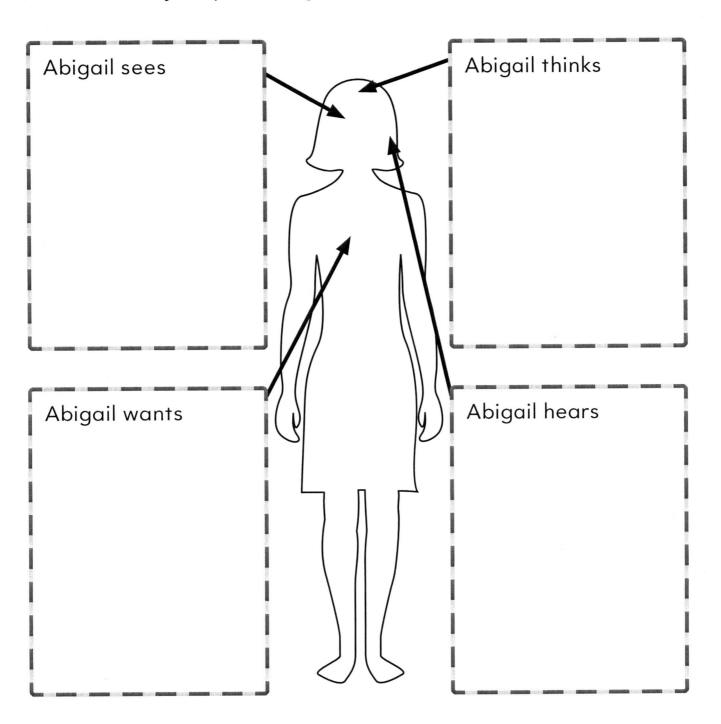

Abigail sees

Abigail thinks

Abigail wants

Abigail hears

★★★ Who's Running? ★★★

Every four years we vote for a new president. But how do we know who is officially running? We find out at the national conventions. They are like big parties! There are even balloons!

Each one is held in the summer before the election. But they are not held at the same time. They last for days. The major political parties each have one.

Lots of people go to these big events. Sometimes, past presidents go! People give speeches. They talk about key issues. They talk about what their party stands for. There is singing. There is music. It is all shown on TV. The whole country can see it.

The fun part is the big announcement. Each party says aloud who will run for president. This person is called the candidate. Most people already know who it is. Yet it is still fun. The crowd goes crazy! People cheer! Everyone gets excited! The people who are chosen give speeches. They want the people to like them. They want to win! They want to be the next president!

Directions: Pretend you are going to one of the national conventions. People usually bring signs to show their support for their candidates. Pick a name for your candidate. Make a sign showing your support for your candidate. Make sure your sign is big, bold, and beautiful!

★★★ **Detailed Balloons** ★★★

Directions: Use both texts to write details about what happens at the national conventions. Write one detail in each balloon.

National Convention

★ ★ ★ **Planning the Perfect Convention** ★ ★ ★

Directions: If you had to plan a national convention, what would you do? Answer the questions below and draw a picture of how your convention will look. Present your plan to the classroom.

1. Where will you have it? List the city and state.

_____

2. Who will you invite to speak on stage?

_____

_____

3. Who will sing and play music?

_____

_____

4. What decorations will you use?

_____

_____

5. What will you feed everyone?

_____

_____

_____

Draw a picture of your convention on a separate sheet of paper.

★★★ Party Time! Primary Source ★★★

Primary Source Background Information

This top picture was taken during the Republican National Convention in September 2008. It took place in St. Paul, Minnesota. Senator John McCain was chosen to be the candidate for the Republican Party. He lost the election that year.

The bottom picture was taken during the Republican National Convention in June 1920. It took place in Chicago, Illinois. Senator Warren G. Harding was chosen to be the candidate for the Republican Party. He won the election that year.

Carol Highsmith, Library of Congress

Moffett Studio and Kauffman & Fabry Co., Library of Congress

★★ Party Time! Primary Source *(cont.)* ★★★

Directions: Look closely at the two pictures of the Republican National Conventions. What is the same? What is different? Write or draw what you notice in the Venn diagram below.

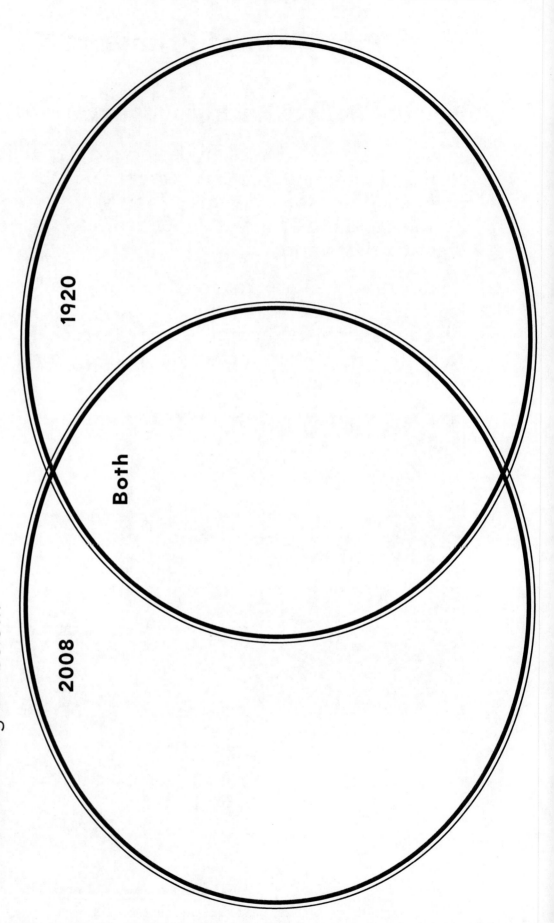

1920

Both

2008

★★ Convention Crossword Vocabulary Puzzle ★★

Directions: Use the clues to complete the puzzle. You can use the words in the Word Bank to help you.

Word Bank

candidate

convention

issues

key

speech

Across

2. You give this when you express and speak your ideas in front of people.

4. These are important topics that people are talking about.

5. This is a person who is trying to be elected.

Down

1. This means "very important."

3. This is a large meeting of people.

★★★ Crazy Convention Puzzle ★★★

Directions: Look closely at the crazy convention picture. Find and circle the pictures of the Word Bank list.

Word Bank

star balloon	podium	cake
crazy straw	dog	police officer

Let's Hit the Road!

Standards

 Students will know examples of situations in which individuals are acting on their own and situations in which individuals' actions are directed by others.

☑ Students will analyze fiction and nonfiction texts and synthesize the information in a variety of ways.

Paired Texts Reading and Activities

★ **You Won't Regret a Vote for Jett** (pages 65–66)—Read the comic aloud while students follow along. Model good fluency. Use different voices for each character. Next, have two student volunteers reread the comic aloud for the class. Then, have students complete page 66 independently to create their own comics based on the one just read.

★ **The Campaign Trail** (page 67)— Read the informational text on page 67 aloud. Then, have students read the text with pencils. Have them circle the things candidates use on the campaign trail to help them get elected (stickers, speeches, etc.). Explain to students that many people who work with candidates volunteer their time. Tell them that leaders direct the volunteers to do what needs to be done. Have students think about times when they act on their own and times when they are told what to do. Then, have students work in pairs to make lists of how they would run campaigns if they were in charge.

★ **Campaigning Counts** (page 68)— Students will use information from both the informational text and the comic to answer text-dependent questions. When students have finished, go over the answers as a class. Have students explain where in the text they found the answers.

★ **Hello from the Road!** (page 69)— With this activity, students will imagine they are on the campaign trail working for a candidate. They will write postcards home that tell what they have been doing on the trail and how they have been helping the candidate. They will draw pictures of where they are on the road on the fronts of the postcards.

Let's Hit the Road! (cont.)

Primary Source Connection

★ **Bring on the Buttons! Primary Source** (pages 70–71)—Study the primary source on page 70 with students. Read the background information to them. Then, have students complete page 71 independently. When students have finished, have them cut out their buttons and wear them for the remainder of the lesson.

Puzzle Time!

★ **Follow the Trail Vocabulary Puzzle** (page 72)—Students will enjoy using the picture clues to help them fill in the missing letters in the vocabulary words.

★ **Crazy Campaign Maze Puzzle** (page 73)—Students will have fun trying to get the candidate to follow the campaign trail to the White House in this crazy maze.

Answer Key

Campaigning Counts (page 68)

1. Candidates travel all over the country. They talk to people and learn what people need and want. They give speeches. They talk and listen to people and shake hands. They pose for pictures, and they go on TV shows.
2. Candidates campaign so people can get to know them better, so they can win people's votes, and so people know what they stand for and what they believe in.
3. Supporters make phone calls. They tell people about their candidate and pass out stickers, buttons, and fliers. They write slogans and make posters and signs.

Bonus: Student answers may vary but could include that voters need to know their candidates well before they vote to make sure they are choosing the right leader for the country.

Hello from the Road! (page 69)

Student postcards will vary, but should be completely filled out.

Follow the Trail Vocabulary Puzzle (page 72)

campaign	flier
sign	slogan
sticker	button

Crazy Campaign Maze Puzzle (page 73)

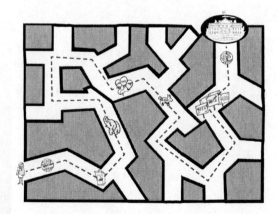

★ ★ ★ You Won't Regret a Vote for Jett ★ ★ ★

★ ★ ★ **You Won't Regret a Vote for Jett** *(cont.)* ★ ★ ★

Directions: Pretend Miss Jett won the election. How would the children in the comic feel? What would they do? Make your own comic below.

★ ★ ★ **The Campaign Trail** ★ ★ ★

Running for president is not easy. You have to campaign. This means that you have to do a lot of different things to win people's votes. You have to travel a lot. It can be very tiring.

If you want to be president you have to travel all over the country. You have to get to know the people. You need to learn what they need. You need to figure out how you can help them if you become president.

You also want people to know who you are. You want them to know what you stand for. You want to make them believe in you. You also want them to like you!

Candidates give speeches. They talk to people. They listen. They shake lots and lots of hands. They pose for pictures. They go on TV shows. They have to prove that they are the best choice.

Candidates are not the only ones working hard. The people who support them work hard, too. These people make phone calls. They tell people about their candidates. They make posters and signs. They give out fliers. They hand out stickers and buttons. They spread the word!

Directions: You are responsible for leading a campaign in your town. You have a group of volunteers to help you. What will you tell your volunteers to do? How will you lead them? How will you spread the word about your candidate? Make a list of what you will do and what your team will do.

★ ★ ★ Campaigning Counts ★ ★ ★

Directions: Use both texts to help you answer the questions below.

1. How do candidates campaign?

_____

_____

2. Why do candidates campaign?

_____

_____

3. How do supporters help candidates campaign?

_____

_____

Bonus!

Why is it important for voters to get to know the candidates before they vote?

_____

_____

★ ★ ★ Hello from the Road! ★ ★ ★

Directions: Pretend you are working for a candidate on the campaign trail. Send a postcard home to your family telling them how you are helping the candidate. Then, draw a picture of where you are in the country for the front of the postcard.

(front)

(back)

To:

_____

_____

_____

★ ★ ★ Bring on the Buttons! Primary Source ★ ★ ★

Primary Source Background Information

Campaign buttons help spread the word. These buttons have been used for a long time. They have been helping candidates for more than 100 years. Do you know which president was the first to have his face put on a button? Did you guess President Lincoln? If you did, you are right! Buttons are still used today! This picture shows a lot of different buttons.

Teresa Azevedo/Shutterstock.com

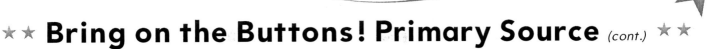

★ ★ **Bring on the Buttons! Primary Source** (cont.) ★ ★

Directions: One classic way to campaign is to make buttons. Some buttons have a candidate's face on them. Others have a slogan or saying. Some have both! Some are funny. Some are serious. Pretend you are running for president. Make some buttons for your campaign. Cut them out and wear them!

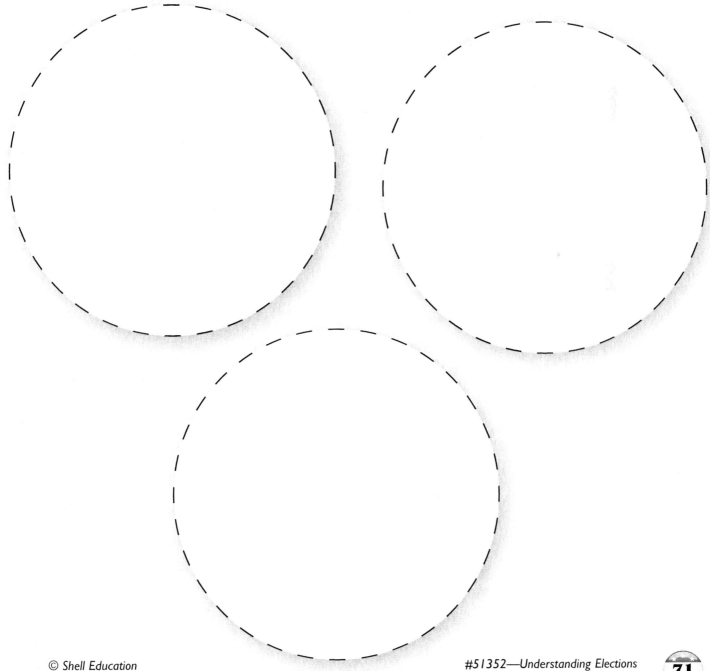

★★★ **Follow the Trail Vocabulary Puzzle** ★★★

Directions: Follow the campaign trail! Fill in the missing letters in the vocabulary words along the way.

c __ m __ a i g __

f __ i e __

__ i g n

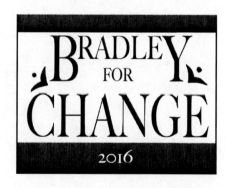

s __ __ g a n

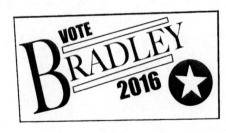

s __ i c k __ __

b __ t __ o n

★★★ Crazy Campaign Maze Puzzle ★★★

Directions: Help the candidate follow the campaign trail to the White House.

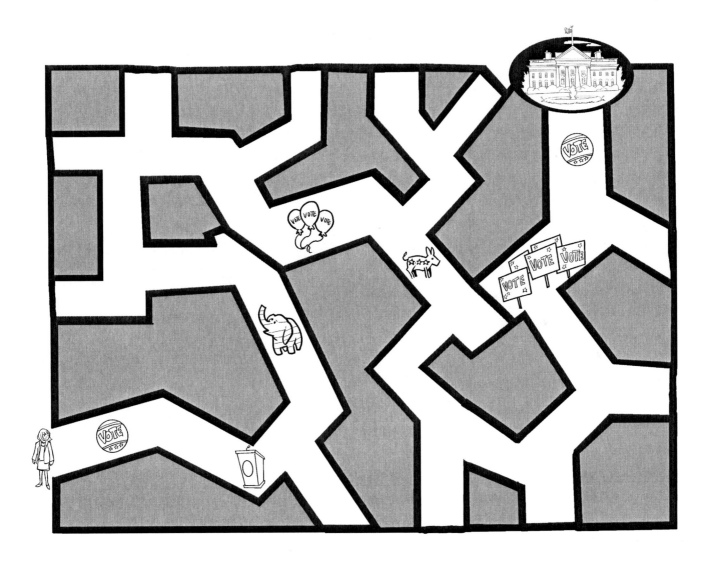

It's Time to Talk

Standards

 Students will know the characteristics of a good leader (e.g., experience, determination, confidence, a desire to be a leader, the ability to solve problems creatively).

 Students will analyze fiction and nonfiction texts and synthesize the information in a variety of ways.

Paired Texts Reading and Activities

★ **Out of this World Debate** (pages 76–77)—Read the science fiction story on page 76 aloud. Model good fluency. Have a class discussion on what makes Steve a good leader and why Marvin may not be the best leader. Then, have students complete page 77 in pairs. When students have finished, go over the graphic organizer as a class.

★ **Let's Talk** (page 78)—Read the informational text on page 78 aloud while students follow along. Then, have students read the text with pencils. Ask students to underline facts about debates. Ask students if they have ever had arguments with others. Ask them how they resolved the arguments and if they won. Have students share their experiences. Explain that debates are controlled arguments in which people clearly state their opinions and have reasons to back up their opinions. Finally, have student pairs debate the issue of homework.

★ **3, 2, 1 Debate!** (page 79)—Students will use information from both the informational text and the science fiction text to list facts and examples. They will also write opinions they have on debates. Students can complete the page individually or in pairs. When students have finished, have volunteers share their responses with the class.

★ **How to Be Great in a Debate** (page 80)—With this activity, students will rate the different skills that can be used in a debate. They will decide which is the best and which is the worst. Have students complete the activity sheet independently and then pair-share their responses.

It's Time to Talk (cont.)

Primary Source Connection

★ **TV Time! Primary Source**
(pages 81–82)—Study the primary
source on page 81 with students.
Read the background information
to them. Then, have students
complete page 82 in pairs. They
will pick topics from the list,
write reasons for why they are for
or against the topics, and then
debate the topics with partners.

Puzzle Time!

★ **The Great Debate Word Find
Vocabulary Puzzle** (page 83)—
Students will enjoy looking closely
to find the hidden vocabulary
words in the puzzle. Be sure
students check off the words as
they find them.

★ **Decoding the Debate Puzzle**
(page 84)—Students will have fun
decoding the secret caption for the
funny picture!

Answer Key

Out of this World Debate (page 77)

Characters: Marvin Nova; Steve Armstrong

Setting: a big hall in New Mexico during election
time at 7 P.M.

Problem: Marvin is an alien and is running
for president

Solution: Steve wins the race and appoints Marvin
head of the space program

3, 2, 1 Debate! (page 79)

Student answers may vary but could include the
following:

3 facts: there are two or more people in a debate;
good debaters speak clearly; debates help you learn
about candidates

2 examples: Marvin and Steve are in a debate; Steve
speaks clearly

1 opinion: I like Marvin. He was just scared people
would find out he was an alien.

TV Time! Primary Source (page 82)

Student notes will differ but should support their
opinion.

The Great Debate Word Find Vocabulary Puzzle
(page 83)

D	O	V	D	E	B	A	T	E	Q
V	R	Q	H	T	O	P	I	C	J
Z	L	U	Y	W	R	J	N	K	I
O	K	E	U	V	A	Y	K	E	S
P	D	S	R	R	R	A	H	Y	S
I	O	T	E	G	G	I	E	M	U
N	V	I	A	I	U	H	C	P	E
I	M	O	S	G	E	Y	W	V	X
O	W	N	O	Y	V	K	B	O	P
N	L	A	N	S	W	E	R	P	L

Decoding the Debate Puzzle (page 84)

Aliens debate in space.

★ ★ ★ Out of this World Debate ★ ★ ★

It was time for the debates. The debate was in New Mexico. It was in a big hall. There were lots of TV cameras. Many people came out to see the event.

The big issue for debate was space travel. Marvin Nova was against space travel. Steve Armstrong was for it. He thought there was a lot to learn from space. Marvin said there was nothing to learn out there.

At 7:00 P.M. the debate began. Steve was great. He had lots of good reasons to explore space. He stayed calm. He spoke clearly. Marvin was not doing so well. He was mad. He was yelling. He kept shouting, "No space travel! No space travel!"

Then Marvin started acting strange. Very strange! He started spinning in a circle. He moved faster and faster. And when he finally stopped he was no longer a man in a suit. He was an alien! The crowd gasped. The people watching on TV could not believe their eyes!

Marvin had scaly skin. It was bright green. He had huge black eyes. He kind of looked like a large lizard. Marvin said he was sorry for tricking everyone. He explained that he was from planet Utapau. He said he loved America. He wanted to stay here. He did not want people to explore space. He was afraid they would find out his secret.

Later that year, Steve won the race. He became president. Marvin could not have won. After all, he was not born here. But, President Steve Armstrong had a special job for Marvin. He is now in charge of the space program!

★ ★ ★ Out of this World Debate (cont.) ★ ★ ★

Directions: Use the science fiction story to complete the graphic organizer below.

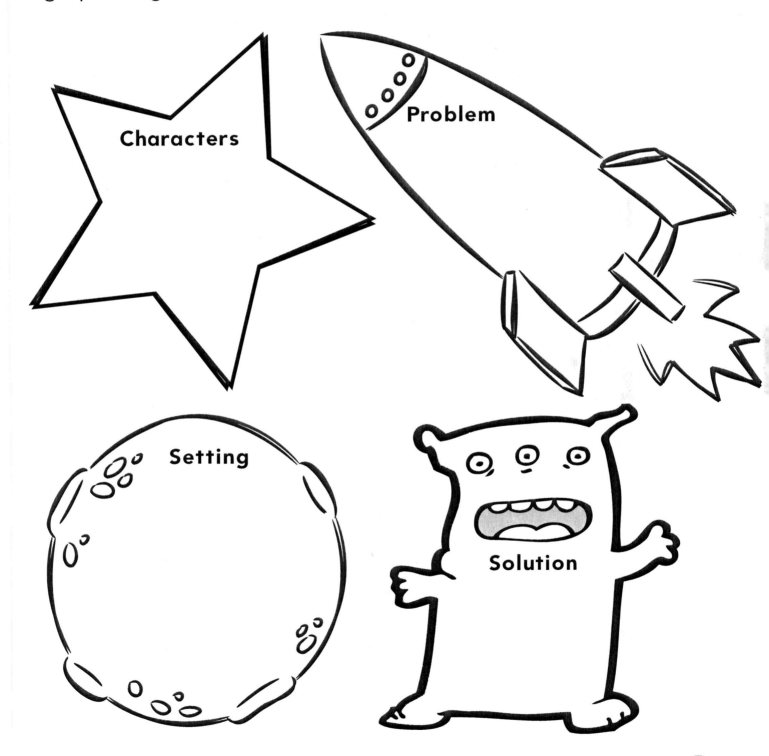

Characters

Problem

Setting

Solution

★★★ Let's Talk ★★★

You must learn all you can about candidates before you vote. This will help you choose the best person to be the next president!

There are many ways to learn about candidates. You can read newspapers. You can read online. Or you can watch TV. You can see ads. You can watch talk shows. One of the best ways is to watch a debate.

In a debate, there are two or more people. They are asked questions. The questions are about key issues. Each person gets time to answer each question. They have a time limit to share their ideas. Each person states his or her opinion. They give reasons for their opinions. They debate until all the key issues are covered.

Good debaters speak clearly. They stay calm. They know their topics well. They give reasons to support their opinions. They use good examples.

Debates help you learn how a candidate thinks and feels. If you think and feel the same way, then you may want to vote for that person. If you do not agree with what the candidate says, then you may want to vote for someone else.

You must watch closely. You must listen carefully. You must think hard. This will help you pick the best person to lead our country.

Directions: Have a debate with a partner about homework! Choose who will be arguing that homework is a good thing. And choose who will be arguing that homework is a bad thing. Let the great debate begin!

★★★ 3, 2, 1 Debate! ★★★

Directions: Write **three** facts you learned from *Let's Talk*. Next, find where **two** of those facts were talked about in *Out of this World Debate.* Then, write **one** opinion you have on debates.

3 facts from *Let's Talk*

1.	2.	3.

2 examples from *Out of this World Debate*

1.	2.

1 opinion on debates

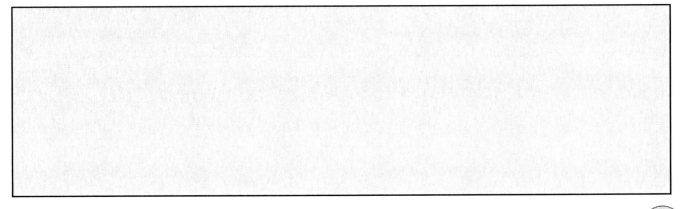

★★★ How to Be Great in a Debate ★★★

Directions: There are many ways to be great in a debate. Read the list of ways to debate. Think about each one. Rate them by how important you think they are. Use the scale below.

4 the best	3 good	2 okay	1 the worst

Ways to Debate	My Rating
speak clearly and slowly	
know your topics very well	
yell your opinions	
give strong reasons to support your opinions	

I think _____

is the best way to debate because _____

_____ .

I think _____

is the worst way to debate because _____

_____ .

★ ★ ★ TV Time! Primary Source ★ ★ ★

Primary Source Background Information

Today you can watch debates on TV. But this was not always the case. The first debate to air on TV was on September 26, 1960. Two men were running for president. There was a young senator. His name was John F. Kennedy. The other man was the vice president of the United States. His name was Richard Nixon. The two men argued back and forth. Kennedy looked fit and young on TV. Nixon looked sweaty and pale. Many people say Kennedy won the debate. They say he won because he looked good on TV. He won the race, too. He became the next president!

Associated Press

★ ★ ★ TV Time! Primary Source (cont.) ★ ★ ★

Directions: Pick one of the topics at the bottom of the page. Cut it out and glue it on the My Notes section. Write reasons why you support the topic or why you are against it. Have a debate with a classmate! Have a few people watch your debate and decide who wins!

My Notes

I think [_____] because . . .

1. _____

   _____

2. _____

   _____

3. _____

   _____

4. _____

   _____

Topics: ★

| dogs are better than cats | kids should get to vote for president |
| recess should be longer | kids should not have cell phones |

★ ★

★★★ The Great Debate Word Find
Vocabulary Puzzle ★★★

Directions: Look closely! Can you find the words listed below in the word puzzle?

answer	issue	question
argue	key	reason
debate	opinion	topic

D	O	V	D	E	B	A	T	E	Q
V	R	Q	H	T	O	P	I	C	J
Z	L	U	Y	W	R	J	N	K	I
O	K	E	U	V	A	Y	K	E	S
P	D	S	R	R	R	A	H	Y	S
I	O	T	E	G	G	I	E	M	U
N	V	I	A	I	U	H	C	P	E
I	M	O	S	G	E	Y	W	V	X
O	W	N	O	Y	V	K	B	O	P
N	L	A	N	S	W	E	R	P	L

Name _____ Date _____

★★★ Decoding the Debate Puzzle ★★★

Directions: Use the key to decode the caption for the picture.

Key

A =	D =	L =	S =
B =	E =	N =	T =
C =	I =	P =	

!

Time to Vote!

Standards

☑ Students will know that a responsibility is a duty to do something or not to do something.

☑ Students will analyze fiction and nonfiction texts and synthesize the information in a variety of ways.

Paired Texts Reading and Activities

★ **Book It to the Booth!**
(pages 87–88)—Read the reader's theater aloud to the class. Model good fluency by changing your voice for each character. Then, have three volunteers read the script aloud. Find out if you have any students who have gone with family members to vote. Have these students share their experiences. Then, have students complete page 88 individually. When they have finished, have students share some of their ideas regarding what good citizens do.

★ **Power to the People** (page 89)—
Read the informational text on page 89 aloud while students follow along. Then, have students read the text with pencils. Ask them to circle words having to do with elections. Have a class discussion on why voting is an important civic duty. Have students share some of their duties at home and at school. Tell students to ask their adult family members or neighbors when they get home about their voting experiences. The next day, have volunteers share what they learned.

★ **Putting It All Together**
(page 90)—Students will use information from both the informational text and the reader's theater to answer the questions of *who, what, when, where, why* and *how*. Encourage students to quote directly from each text and have them add as much information as they can to the graphic organizer. Students can complete the page individually or in pairs. When students have finished, have volunteers share their responses with the class.

★ **Build Your Perfect Candidate**
(page 91)—With this activity, students will build their ideal candidate by cutting out body parts and gluing them together. Each body part has a characteristic on it. Go over all the characteristics as a class before students begin assembling their candidates. Have students complete the activity sheet independently and then pair-share their responses.

Time to Vote! *(cont.)*

Primary Source Connection

★ **A President Votes Primary Source** (pages 92–93)—Study the primary source on page 92 with students. Read the background information to them. Then, have students complete page 93 individually. They will vote to create their first election. When students have finished, tally the votes to see which Election Day choices were the most popular.

Puzzle Time!

★ **Getting Help from the Grid Vocabulary Puzzle** (page 94)— Students will enjoy using a grid to match up vocabulary words with their definitions.

★ **Help the President Puzzle** (page 95)—Students will have fun getting President Roosevelt through the maze so that he can cast his vote!

Answer Key

Putting It All Together (page 90)

Who: Mom, Nora, Leo; voters

What: People vote.

When: Some people go in the morning; some people go at lunch; some people go in the evening.

Where: community clubhouse

Why: People vote to be responsible, to be good citizens, and to pick great leaders for the country.

How: You can vote using a paper ballot, a machine, or a computer.

Build Your Perfect Candidate (page 91)

Student candidates will differ but should include five of the qualities listed.

Getting Help from the Grid Vocabulary Puzzle (page 94)

1. duty   3. polling place   5. booth

2. cast   4. private   6. research

Help the President Puzzle (page 95)

★ ★ ★ **Book It to the Booth!** ★ ★ ★

Mom:	*(calling loudly)* What are you kids doing up there? Let's go! You're going to be late for school, and I'm going to be late for work!
Nora:	*(calling loudly)* It's only 7, Mom!
Leo:	*(calling loudly)* Yeah, we have lots of time.
Mom:	No, we don't because I have to vote before I take you to school. Get in the car, please. We need to go to the community clubhouse. That's where the polling place is.
Nora:	Ugh. Why do you have to vote at all?
Leo:	Yeah, it's not like you'll go to jail if you don't vote.
Mom:	Because I care who the president is. Would you like it if someone who wasn't smart were in charge?
Nora:	No. I would be scared that our country wouldn't be safe.
Mom:	Would you like it if a mean person were in charge?
Leo:	*(sighing)* No. That wouldn't be good, either.
Mom:	Not all countries get to pick their leaders. We are lucky that we do. It is my duty as a good citizen to vote.
Nora:	Mom, why do you have to go in that booth to vote?
Leo:	Because it's private! Right, mom?
Mom:	That's right! Voting in privacy is a right. It's the law. This way, I can vote for whomever I like. And I won't feel pressure from people to vote for someone I don't like.
Nora:	I hope the person you vote for wins, Mom!
Leo:	Me too!
Mom:	Me three!

Name _____ Date _____

★ ★ ★ Book It to the Booth! *(cont.)* ★ ★ ★

Directions: Voting is a duty. It is a responsibility. Good citizens vote. What else do good citizens do? Think of four more things that good citizens do, and draw them below.

Good Citizens

★ ★

★ ★

★★★ Power to the People ★★★

The big day is here! It's Tuesday. It's Election Day! It is time for the people to use their power and vote. It is time to pick a new president.

By Election Day, most people know whom they will vote for. They have done a lot of research. They know their candidate well. They know what makes that person a good choice.

At the polling place, you give your name and address. You may have to sign your name on a sheet of paper. Then, you will be handed a ballot. If you are voting on a computer, you may be handed a number.

Next, you go into a voting booth. This keeps your votes private. No one will know whom you vote for. It will be a secret. This way, you cannot be bullied or pressured to vote for someone you do not like.

You may use a machine to vote. Or you may use a computer. When you are finished, you may put your ballot into a box. Or, you may push a submit button. That's it! You have cast your vote!

After you vote, you get a sticker. The sticker says, "I voted!" It is important to vote. It is a civic duty. It means you are a good citizen. It means you care about your country.

Directions: When you go home tonight, ask your adult family members these questions. They will help you learn more about how your local elections work. Where is your polling place located? Do you vote on paper, with a machine, or on a computer?

★ ★ ★ **Putting It All Together** ★ ★ ★

Directions: Use text from both the reader's theater and the nonfiction text to fill in the graphic organizer below. Include as much information as you can!

Who goes to the polling place?	**What** happens at the polling place?	**When** do people go to the polling place?
Where is the polling place?	**Why** do people vote?	**How** do people vote?

Name _____ Date _____

★★★ **Build Your Perfect Candidate** ★★★

Directions: Think about your perfect candidate. What kind of person would you vote for to be president? Choose five qualities from the Word Bank. Then, draw arrows from those qualitites to the candidate below.

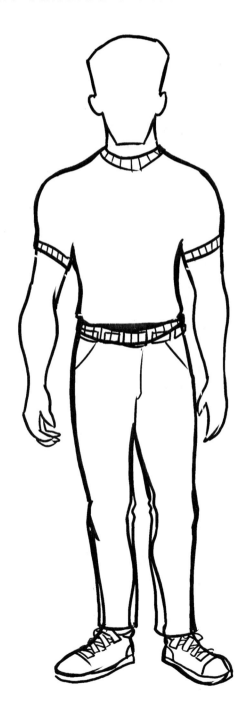

Word Bank

- wise and caring
- good problem-solver
- listens well
- wants more taxes
- helps the environment
- smart and honest
- lots of experience
- helps people
- speaks well
- wants fewer taxes

★★★ A President Votes Primary Source ★★★

Primary Source Background Information

This picture was taken November 6, 1934. It was a Tuesday. It shows President Franklin D. Roosevelt. He is coming out of a voting booth. He had just voted. He wanted to be a good citizen. He felt it was his civic duty. There was no voting for a president in this election. But Roosevelt did vote for other leaders in our country.

© Bettmann/CORBIS

#51352—Understanding Elections   © Shell Education

★ ★ ★ A President Votes Primary Source (cont.) ★ ★ ★

Directions: How do you want your first election to go? Vote for your favorite options below to create your dream election. Then, on the back of this sheet, draw a picture of you voting in your first election.

I will vote . . .

☐ in the morning.

☐ in the afternoon.

☐ late at night.

I will vote using . . .

☐ a machine.

☐ a computer.

☐ a high-tech tablet.

I will get to the polling place by . . .

☐ walking.

☐ driving.

☐ flying.

My polling place will be . . .

☐ in a clubhouse.

☐ in a town hall.

☐ in outer space.

★★★ **Getting Help from the Grid Vocabulary Puzzle** ★★★

Directions: Use the grid to help you find the correct vocabulary word for each definition.

	A	**B**	**C**
1	duty	booth	cast
2	research	polling place	private

1. _____ —something you do because it is the right thing to do (A, 1)

2. _____ —to turn in a vote (C, 1)

3. _____ —the place where people vote (B, 2)

4. _____ —not public (C, 2)

5. _____ —a small private space to vote (B, 1)

6. _____ —finding information about a subject (A, 2)

★ ★ ★ Help the President Puzzle ★ ★ ★

Directions: Be a good citizen and help President Roosevelt travel from the White House to his polling place to vote. He needs to fulfill his civic duty!

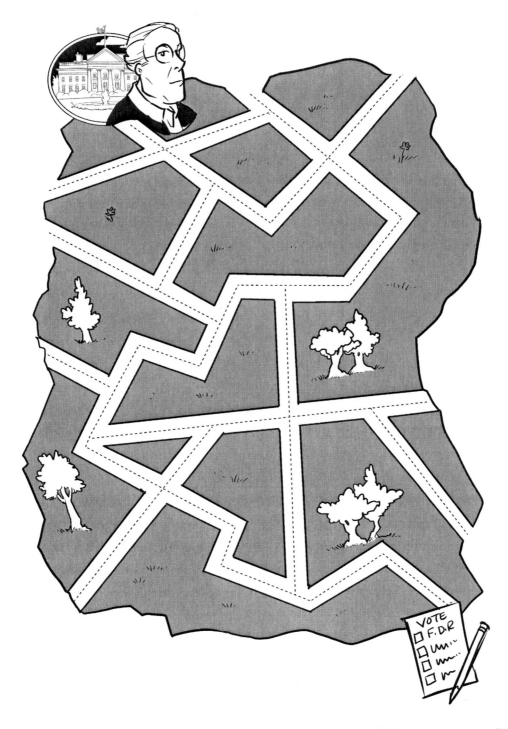

Count Them!

Standards

☑ Students will know that procedural justice refers to problems arising over fair ways to gather information and make just decisions, and know examples of situations involving procedural justice (e.g., how a class president should go about deciding which games the class will play).

☑ Students will analyze fiction and nonfiction texts and synthesize the information in a variety of ways.

Paired Texts Reading and Activities

★ **The Mystery of the Missing Votes** (pages 98–99)—Read the mystery fiction text aloud to the class. Find out if you have any students who have read a mystery story or watched a mystery movie. Have these students share their experiences. Then, have students complete page 99 individually. When they have finished, have them shout out together the mystery object.

★ **The Polls Are Closed** (page 100)— Read the informational text on page 100 aloud. Then, have students read the text with pencils. Ask them to circle any words they do not understand. Have a class discussion to clarify these words. Tell students they are going to conduct polls at home. Have them ask 10 family members and/or friends which they like better: reading or watching TV. Have students keep track of the "votes" on paper. Have them count the votes and report the final counts the next day in class. Tally the votes on the board and add the final numbers as a class to find out the "winner."

★ **Piece It Together** (page 101)— Students will use information from the informational text to complete the graphic organizer. They will determine the main idea of the text and list the details that support it. Encourage students to quote directly from the text. Students will also answer a question about *The Mystery of the Missing Votes* text. Students can complete the page individually or in pairs. When they have finished, have volunteers share their responses with the class.

★ **Your Turn to Count** (page 102)—With this activity, students will vote using ballots. You will need to have a ballot box ready to collect these ballots. After students have cast their votes, place students in small groups. Give each group a handful of ballots from the box. Have the groups count the votes using the table at the bottom of the page. Ask each group to submit its final count to you. Tally the final counts as a class and declare a winner.

Count Them! *(cont.)*

Primary Source Connection

★ **Counting the Votes Primary Source** (pages 103–104)— Study the primary source on page 103 with students. Read the background information to them. Have students complete the Venn diagram on page 104 in small groups. They will compare and contrast counting votes in 1876 and today. When groups have finished their Venn diagrams, have each student draw a modern-day version of the 1876 picture.

Puzzle Time!

★ **Mystery Word Vocabulary Puzzle** (page 105)—Students will enjoy using context clues to guess the mystery vocabulary word. Challenge students to create their own mystery word vocabulary puzzles.

★ **Polling Place Puzzle** (page 106)— Students will have fun studying the silly pictures closely and finding the hidden differences between the two.

Answer Key

The Mystery of the Missing Votes (page 99)

ballot box

Piece It Together (page 101)

Main idea: how votes are counted in elections

Details: Long ago, it took a long time to count votes, but today it is faster. Machines and computers help count votes. Officials need to look at paper ballots closely. The news reports the winner.

Question: A different candidate could have won the election.

Counting the Votes Primary Source (page 104)

Student answers will vary but may include the following:

1876: They are counting votes by hand

Today: There are computers and machines

Both: people helping to count votes

Mystery Word Vocabulary Puzzle (page 105)

  1. officials   2. results   3. winner

Challenge: Answers will vary but should include context clues.

Polling Place Puzzle (page 106)

★ ★ ★ The Mystery of the Missing Votes ★ ★ ★

Election Day had ended. The Hound Hill City officials counted the votes carefully. But what they found shocked them. There were ballots missing! They counted the ballots again. There were 314 ballots. But 316 people had voted. Two ballots were gone!

The officials called for help. Detective Brown soon arrived with his dog, Sherlock. Sherlock was a hound dog. He was good at sniffing out clues. Sherlock began sniffing. First, he sniffed the ballot box. Then, he sniffed all around the floor in the city hall. It wasn't long before Sherlock started barking loudly. He was barking at a small hole in the wall. It was near the floor. "Ruff, ruff, ruff!" barked Sherlock.

Detective Brown got down on the floor. He shined a light into the hole. He could not believe his eyes. There in the tiny hole was a tiny mouse. She had just finished making a new cozy nest. And what had she used to make her new nest? The missing ballots!

Detective Brown pulled the ballots out of the wall. Then, he studied the ballot box. There in the bottom of the box was a small hole. Detective Brown proudly stated, "This mouse is the thief. She chewed a hole in the ballot box. Next, she took two of the ballots. She used them to make a nest. Case solved!"

"Ruff!" barked Sherlock, smiling.

The missing votes were counted. That night, a new president was elected. As for the mouse, one of the officials took her home. She kept the mouse as a pet. She named the mouse after the new president!

★ ★ ★ The Mystery of the Missing Votes (cont.) ★ ★ ★

Directions: Detective Brown and his dog, Sherlock, solved the mystery of the missing votes. Now, it's your turn to solve a mystery. Use the clues listed below to guess the mystery object. When you think you know what the object is, draw a picture of it.

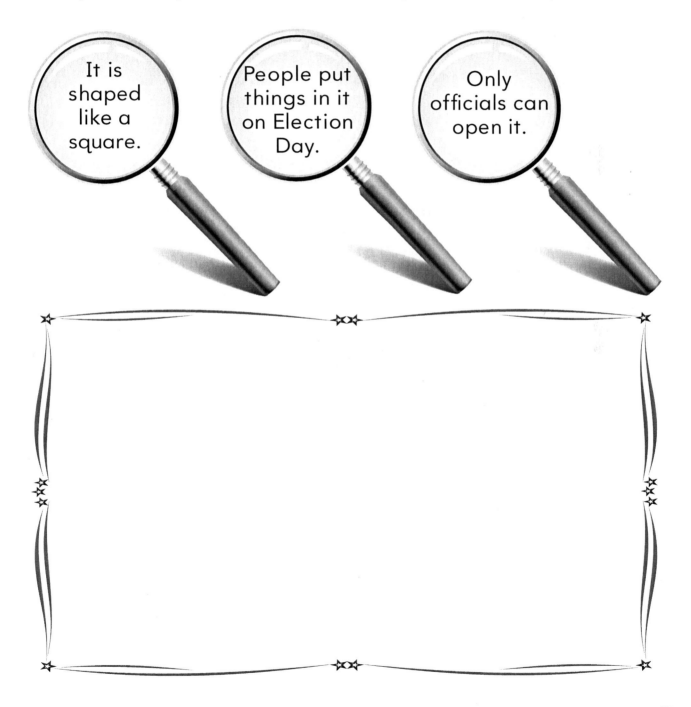

It is shaped like a square.

People put things in it on Election Day.

Only officials can open it.

★ ★ ★ The Polls Are Closed ★ ★ ★

It is dark outside. The polling places are closed. What happens next? It is time to count!

Long ago, it took a lot of time to count votes. People would have to sort them by hand. Then, they would have to add them all up. Sometimes, it would take weeks before people knew who had won.

Today, everything is much faster! We have machines to help. And we have computers! We still need people to help, too. These people are called *officials*.

Some polling places use paper ballots. Officials need to check these. They look at them closely. They make sure people did not make mistakes. Sometimes, a person may vote for two candidates for the same job. When this happens, the vote does not count. After they check the ballots, the officials put them in a machine. It counts the votes for them.

Some polling places have computers. This makes it easier. Officials just have to click the mouse a few times. Then, they get the results. They do not need to check the ballots. And they do not have to put them in a machine.

The votes have all been counted. The officials now have the final numbers. The winner is announced on the news. Now, everyone knows who the next president will be!

Directions: When you go home tonight, ask your friends and family if they like reading or watching TV more. Have them vote for one or the other. Keep track of the votes on a sheet of paper. After you have asked ten people, count the votes. Report your winner in class tomorrow.

★ ★ ★ **Piece It Together** ★ ★ ★

Directions: Use *The Polls Are Closed* text to complete the graphic organizer below. Write the main idea of the text on the line. Then, list the details that support the main idea in the puzzle pieces. Finally, answer the question at the bottom of the page.

Main Idea: _____

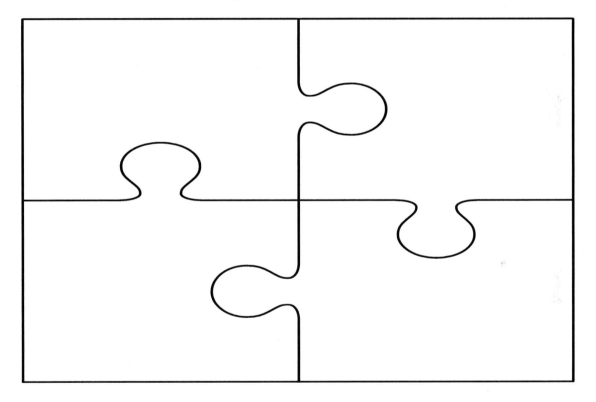

Question: Think about *The Mystery of the Missing Votes* story. What may have happened if those two votes had not been counted?

_____

_____

_____

★★★ **Your Turn to Count** ★★★

Directions: Cut out the ballot below. Place a check in a box to vote. If you do not like the choices, you can write in your own choice on the line. Place your vote in the ballot box.

Ballot

What is your favorite kind of pet?

❑ bird   ❑ cat   ❑ dog   ❑ _____

Directions: Use the table below to count your group's votes. Add a tally mark for each vote in the correct row. Then, count the tally marks.

Pet	Tally	Total
bird		
cat		
dog		

★ ★ ★ Counting the Votes Primary Source ★ ★ ★

Primary Source Background Information

This picture is from November 7, 1876. It shows officials counting ballots. The two candidates were Samuel J. Tilden and Rutherford B. Hayes. There were problems in this election. Many people said the votes were not counted fairly. In some states, the votes had to be counted again. It took almost four months to find out who won. In March 1877, Hayes was announced as the winner.

S.W. Bennett, Library of Congress

★★★ Counting the Votes Primary Source *(cont.)* ★★ ★

Directions: Look at the picture of the men counting votes in 1876. How is this picture different from how votes are counted today? How is it the same? Fill out the Venn diagram below. Then, draw what this picture would look like today on a separate sheet of paper.

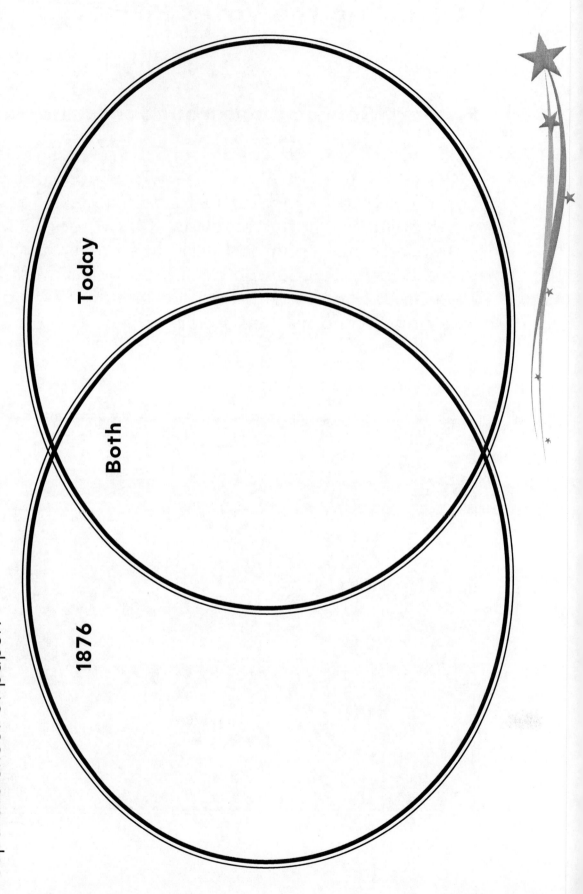

Today

Both

1876

★★★ **Mystery Word Vocabulary Puzzle** ★★★

Directions: Read the text. Use the context clues to help you figure out each mystery word. Circle the correct word for each mixed-up word.

1. The <u>calisofif</u> have an important job on Election Day. It is up to the <u>calisofif</u> to count the votes. The <u>calisofif</u> know what the final numbers are.

   presidents   **officials**   **candidates**

2. The <u>stulser</u> tell you who won. You don't know the <u>stulser</u> until all the votes are counted. The news tells everyone the <u>stulser</u>.

   results   **officials**   **winners**

3. After the votes are counted, the <u>newnir</u> is announced. The person with the most votes is the <u>newnir</u>. The <u>newnir</u> becomes the new president.

   president   **candidate**   **winner**

Challenge: Write your own sentences with a mystery word. Remember to give context clues that your partner can follow to figure out the mystery word!

_____

_____

_____

★★★ Polling Place Puzzle ★★★

Directions: Look at both pictures closely. Do you see any differences between the two pictures? Circle the seven differences that you see.

© Shell Education

Let's Celebrate!

 Standards

 Students know the benefits of fulfilling responsibilities.

 Students will analyze fiction and nonfiction texts and synthesize the information in a variety of ways.

Paired Texts Reading and Activities

★ **Crowds Pack Downtown D.C.** (pages 109–110)—Read the fictional newspaper article on page 109 aloud to the class. Ask students if they have ever fulfilled a responsibility such as a chore or task. Ask them what the result was. Ask if their parents praised them or if they earned a reward. Have students share their experiences. Explain that candidates fulfill many responsibilities. They work very hard, and for some, the benefit is becoming president. Have students complete page 110 individually. Read aloud some of the students' responses.

★ **A Long Day** (page 111)—Read the informational text on page 111 aloud while students follow along. Then, have students read the text with pencils. Ask them to circle all the times in the text. Create a timeline of events on the board with students. Ask any students who have ever had very busy days to share their experiences with the class. Then, have students work in small groups to draw their tips.

★ **Busy Schedule** (page 112)— Students will use information from both the informational text and fictional news article to complete the page. They will fill in the missing pieces in the president's busy schedule. Students can complete the page individually or in pairs. When students have finished, go over the schedule as a class.

★ **My Big Day** (page 113)—With this activity, students will imagine they are becoming the next president. They will visualize what their Inauguration Day will be like. They will decide what to wear, what they will talk about in their speeches, what their parade will have, and who they will invite. Then, students will draw a few pictures from their big day. Have student volunteers share these pictures with the class.

Let's Celebrate! *(cont.)*

Primary Source Connection

★ **A Letter to the New President Primary Source** (pages 114–115)—Study the primary source on page 114 with students. Read the letter aloud. Read the background information to them. Then, have students complete page 115. They will write letters to a new president showing their support and giving encouragement. When students have finished, share a few of their letters with the class.

Puzzle Time!

★ **Match-Up Vocabulary Puzzle** (page 116)—Students will enjoy drawing different colored lines to connect each image with the correct vocabulary word.

★ **Riddle Me This Inauguration Day Puzzle** (page 117)—Students will have fun trying to solve the riddle by deciding if statements about Inauguration Day are true or false. If they choose correctly, the answers will solve the riddle!

Answer Key

Busy Schedule (page 112)

9:30 A.M.: ceremony begins

12:00 P.M.: president takes oath

12:30 P.M.: president's speech

1:00 P.M.: ceremony ends

3:00 P.M.: parade begins

6:00 P.M.: ball begins

Match-Up Vocabulary Puzzle (page 116)

Riddle Me This Inauguration Day Puzzle (page 117)

1. T (true)
2. E (true)
3. D (false)
4. D (true)
5. Y (false)

Teddy Roosevelt

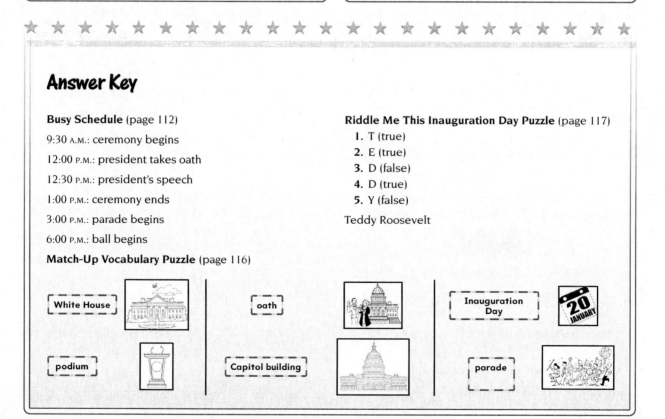

★ ★ ★ Crowds Pack Downtown D.C. ★ ★ ★

By Currer Bell
Freedom Press Staff Writer

Washington, D.C.—It was a fiercely cold day. But one filled with sunshine. More than one million people filled the streets of D.C. They were all there to see the new president.

The day started at the Capitol building. The U.S. Army Band played. The vice president took his oath. He promised to perform his duties. Then, it was the president's turn.

Anthony Martinez stepped forward. He raised his hand. He took the oath. He promised he would do his best. He would follow the laws. He would defend the Constitution.

Next, Mary Anderson performed. She is President Martinez's favorite singer. She sang "America the Beautiful." Then, it was time for the big speech.

President Martinez walked to the podium. The crowd roared. He looked around. Everyone was cheering. He took a deep breath. The crowd got quiet. He began to speak.

He said he was not there to celebrate his win. He was there to celebrate freedom. He was thrilled to live in a free country. "In our country people choose their leaders," he said, "and I am proud that my country chose me."

Next, pop star Selfie sang "The Star-Spangled Banner." Afterwards, President Martinez signed official documents. But his day did not end there! He still had a private lunch at the Capitol. Then, there was a big parade. And, who could forget the balls that night? Let's hope he had comfortable shoes to wear!

★★★ Crowds Pack Downtown D.C. *(cont.)* ★★★

Directions: One of the most important parts of Inauguration Day is the speech. If you were the new president, what would you say? Fill in the blanks below to write your speech.

My fellow citizens,

I promise to _____

_____

_____ .

I will help _____

_____

_____ .

I will change _____

_____

_____

I will protect _____

_____

_____

★★★ A Long Day ★★★

Inauguration means "a formal event." Inauguration Day is in January. It happens every four years. It is a long but fun day! On that day, the new president takes over.

Around 9 A.M. people start to gather. They meet at the Capitol Building. This is in Washington, D.C. It is also where the new president takes the oath. This happens around 12 P.M.

An oath is a promise. Presidents promise to do the best job they can. They promise to follow the laws. They promise to protect the Constitution. Then, they give a big speech.

During the event, bands play. Singers sing. A poet may read a poem. People are excited for the new president. This part of the day ends around 1 P.M.

Later, there is a huge parade. This happens around 3 P.M. The new president walks or rides in a car. The parade goes down Pennsylvania Avenue. It stops at the White House.

Around 6 P.M., there are balls. These are big fancy parties. There is dinner and dancing. When they are over, the president can go to the White House!

Directions: Inauguration Day is a long day for a new president. He or she has lots to do that day. Can you think of some tips or tricks that would help the new president get through the day? Work in a small group to create a picture that shows your tips.

★★★ Busy Schedule ★★★

Directions: Use both texts to help you fill in the missing pieces in the busy schedule below. Cut apart the pieces at the bottom of the page and glue them in the correct spots.

January 20

9:00 A.M.	arrive at the Capitol building
9:30 A.M.	
10:30 A.M.	band plays
11:00 A.M.	poem read
12:00 P.M.	
12:30 P.M.	
12:50 P.M.	song
1:00 P.M.	
1:30 P.M.	private lunch
3:00 P.M.	
6:00 P.M.	
7:30 P.M.	dinner served
8:00 P.M.	dancing
11:00 P.M.	balls end

ceremony begins	balls begin	president's speech
ceremony ends	parade begins	president takes oath

★★★ My Big Day ★★★

Directions: You just got elected president! Now, you have to get ready for your Inauguration Day! What will you wear? What will you talk about in your speech? What will be in the parade? Who will you invite to the ball?

I will wear _____

_____

_____

_____

_____

_____

I will talk about _____

_____

_____

_____

_____

_____

My parade will have _____

_____

_____

_____

_____

_____

I will invite _____

_____

_____

_____

_____

_____

Bonus: On the back of this sheet, draw pictures from your Inauguration Day!

★★★ A Letter to the New President
Primary Source ★★★

Primary Source Background Information

On January 20, 1961, a young man became president. His name was John F. Kennedy. He was 43 years old. It was very cold that day. There was lots of snow on the ground. But that did not stop anyone. Lots of people came out to see the new president. Even more people saw him on TV. It was the first inauguration to be on TV. Brenda was at school. She was in third grade. She watched it on TV. She wrote this letter to the new president. She wanted to wish him luck in his new job.

Kendall Home School
Rt. 4 Box 1090
Miami, Fla

Dear President John F. Kennedy,

   We saw you on T.V. when you were inaugurated. We wished you would put on your coat, so you wouldn't get a cold.

   Mrs. Hansen is our teacher, and she brought her portable T.V. We watched the parade, too.

   We know you will be our best President, and wish you good luck.

   Love to Caroline and John Jr.

      Love
      Brenda Sue Warren
      3 grade.

John F. Kennedy Presidential Library and Museum

★ ★ ★ A Letter to the New President
Primary Source *(cont.)* ★ ★ ★

Directions: Imagine there is a new president. You want to write and encourage the president to do his or her best. What would you write? How would you support the new president? Write your letter below.

Dear _____ ,

Name _____ Date _____

★★★ Match-Up Vocabulary Puzzle ★★★

Directions: Match the vocabulary word to the correct picture by drawing a line. Use a different color crayon or marker for each line.

White House

podium

oath

Capitol building

Inauguration Day

parade

★ ★ ★ **Riddle Me This Inauguration Day Puzzle** ★ ★ ★

Directions: Many things happen on Inauguration Day. Read the statements below. Choose if they are true or false by circling the letter in the correct column. Then, write the letters you circled in order at the bottom of the page. They will tell you the answer to the riddle!

	True	False
1. On this day, the new president takes an oath.	T	F
2. On this day, the new president gives a speech.	E	R
3. On this day, the new president votes.	A	D
4. On this day, there is a fancy ball.	D	N
5. This day takes place in July in the summer.	K	Y

I was the youngest man to become president.

Who am I?

_____ _____ _____ _____ _____   Roosevelt

Culminating Activity—Classroom Election

As students have learned, elections are a fair and just way to choose new laws and leaders. Give students a chance to participate in a mock election. Follow the steps below.

Materials

- ★ copies of *Voter Registration Card* (page 120)
- ★ copies of *Ballot* (page 120)
- ★ copies of *Votes for the President* (page 120)

- ★ two different teddy bears
- ★ art supplies
- ★ ballot box
- ★ patriotic decorations, music, and snacks (*optional*)

Step 1

Tell students there will be a pretend presidential election this week! Tell students two candidates are running in the election: Fuzzy Bear and Brown Bear. Recreate the table below on the board. Go over each candidate with the students. Answer any questions students may have. Tell students to take their time and really think about which bear will make the best leader for their country.

	Fuzzy Bear	**Brown Bear**
Experience	senator	mayor
Characteristics	kind, smart, good at helping people	honest, hard worker, problem solver
Beliefs	the government should help people by providing services wants to raise taxes to help those in need	the government should encourage people to help themselves and be independent wants to lower taxes

Step 2

Give one *Voter Registration Card* to each student. Have students fill out the cards by writing their names, addresses, and drawing pictures of themselves. Explain to students that before you can vote in an election, you have to register.

Culminating Activity—Classroom Election (cont.)

Step 3

Have students help make campaign posters and buttons, using art supplies. Tell students that they can make posters or buttons for either bear, but that does not mean that he or she needs to vote for that bear. Hang the posters around the room. If students would like, have them tape their buttons to their clothes to show their support for their candidates.

Step 4

Have students vote for their candidate on copies of the B*allot* (page 120). Be sure you have one for each student. Set up one or two private spots (voting booths) in the back of the room. Have students vote one or two at a time. After they fill out their ballots, have them cast their votes by placing the ballots in the ballot box.

Step 5

Count the votes as a class. Distribute copies of the *Votes for the President* table (page 120). Read the votes aloud as students mark the results on their tables. Declare a winner! If time permits, have an Inauguration Day celebration! Decorate the room in patriotic colors. Serve tasty snacks. Play patriotic music. Dance and sing. Have fun, and celebrate the newly elected president!

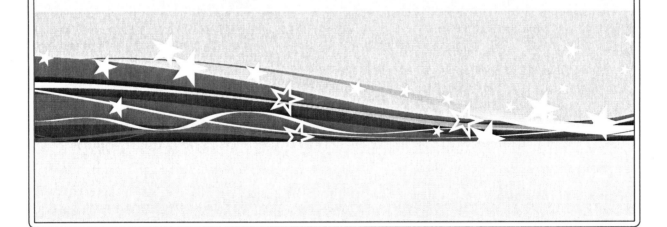

Culminating Activity—Classroom Election (cont.)

Voter Registration Card

Date of Issue:

_____

Name:

_____

Address:_____

_____

Voting Site:_____

_____

Ballot

★★★★★ **President** ★★★★★

❏ Fuzzy Bear
❏ Brown Bear

Votes for the President

Directions: Color a rectangle next to the candidate's name each time a vote for that candidate is read aloud. Count the votes to see who is the winner.

	1	2	3	4	5	6	7	8	9	10	11	12	13	14	15	16	17	18	19	20
Fuzzy Bear																				
Brown Bear																				